T0312297

Cambridge Elements

Elements in Business Strategy
edited by
J.-C. Spender
Kozminski University

DYNAMIC CAPABILITIES

History and an Extension

Bart Nooteboom

Tilburg University

CAMBRIDGE
UNIVERSITY PRESS

University Printing House, Cambridge CB2 8BS, United Kingdom

One Liberty Plaza, 20th Floor, New York, NY 10006, USA

477 Williamstown Road, Port Melbourne, VIC 3207, Australia

314–321, 3rd Floor, Plot 3, Splendor Forum, Jasola District Centre, New Delhi – 110025, India

103 Penang Road, #05–06/07, Visioncrest Commercial, Singapore 238467

Cambridge University Press is part of the University of Cambridge.

It furthers the University's mission by disseminating knowledge in the pursuit of education, learning, and research at the highest international levels of excellence.

www.cambridge.org
Information on this title: www.cambridge.org/9781009014182
DOI: 10.1017/9781009029025

© Bart Nooteboom 2022

First published 2022

A catalogue record for this publication is available from the British Library.

ISBN 978-1-009-01418-2 Paperback
ISSN 2515-0693 (online)
ISSN 2515-0685 (print)

Dynamic Capabilities

History and an Extension

Elements in Business Strategy

DOI: 10.1017/9781009029025
First published online: July 2022

Bart Nooteboom
Tilburg University

Author for correspondence: *Bart Nooteboom*, Bart.nooteboom@gmail.com

Abstract: The development of salient ideas and publications on dynamic capabilities is given in this Element, extended by ideas outside the literature of strategic management. Dynamic capability is presented as an interdisciplinary subject to which knowledge is central. Diversity of knowledge is treated in terms of cognitive distance, limited through organisational focus. To deal with diversity, development and uncertainty, evolutionary theory and the notion of entropy are used. The relation between individual and organisational knowledge is modelled with the notion of a script and linguistic ideas. The governance of collaborative relations for innovation is discussed, including trust, as these are also dynamic capabilities.

Keywords: dynamic capabilities, innovation, strategic management, learning

ISBNs: 9781009014182 (PB), 9781009029025 (OC)
ISSNs: 2515-0693 (online), 2515-0685 (print)

Contents

1 Dynamic Capabilities

1.1 Concepts and Findings

Dynamic capabilities (DCs) are an aspect of strategic management (SM). Strategy entails that in decision-making one anticipates an intelligent opponent's actions and reactions. Interaction with others is therefore a key feature of strategy. In economics, strategic thinking spawned game theory. The term 'strategy' often falls into hyperbole. I once heard someone say that they were going to figure out their strategy for travelling to Amsterdam. With the railway service hardly being an intelligent opponent, they were of course just mapping their journey.

Strategic management is strategy in organisational policy. First, it was based on the structure-conduct-performance (SCP) paradigm from industrial economics (IE). Industrial economics is meso-economics, between micro and macro: the economics of industries, markets and institutions. Strategic management was therefore seen as external in positioning the firm in its competitive environment. The SCP paradigm is compactly presented by Michael Porter's (1980) 'five forces model', with internal rivalry in the industry, vertical rivalry with suppliers and customers and horizontal rivalry with institutions and competing industries. It states that in their positioning, firms should adjust to changes in their environment, but it is static in that it does not include entrepreneurship and innovation, and there is no attention to what happens inside the firm or to differences between firms in an industry. However, the issue of positioning in the competitive environment remains relevant.

Subsequently, SM turned to firms' internal resources with resource-based theory (RBT) (Wernerfelt, 1995; Barney, 2001; Kraaijenbrink *et al.*, 2010). That was still static, and entrepreneurship and innovation were still separate fields. Penrose (1959), however, held that it is not the resources that matter but their arrangement and exploitation. Separate resources are often imitable, but their composition is distinctive, yielding competitive advantage. This represented a shift in attention to diversity: organisations and people in them differ. The old economic notions of 'the representative firm' in an industry and a homogeneous labour force as a factor of production were left behind. This led to the competence-based view, which in turn spawned the dynamic capabilities view. Dynamic capabilities are, simply, the capabilities of successfully performing entrepreneurial innovation to achieve competitive advantage.

In its attention to entrepreneurship, the literature on DC is related to Austrian economics (e.g. Hayek, 1945), with its attention to action, praxeology (Lachmann, 1978) and entrepreneurship (Kirzner, 1973). That has its basis in methodological individualism, with the assumption of full rationality and subjective individual valuation that becomes objectified collectively in a price, causing an equilibrium of supply and demand. Austrian economics accepts that uncertainty is key in innovation. Uncertainty is distinguished from risk, where one does not know what will happen but one can anticipate what *can* happen so that one can attach probabilities to possible events and outcomes, and calculate expected outcomes. Under uncertainty one does *not* know all that can happen. One can hypothesise possible futures and conditions and conduct scenario analyses, investigating which policies perform best in each of those futures. One can then see which are robust, yielding reasonable but not necessarily optimal outcomes across those futures. Scenario planning is a DC for dealing with uncertainty. Austrian economics takes an evolutionary view in that firms place bets on the future and are selected out in the market when failing. In the following I will adopt such evolutionary theory.

Methodological individualism, generally adopted in economics, is opposed to the methodological collectivism purportedly ruling in sociology. There is an intermediate position of methodological inter-actionism, where people develop and adapt their identities and thoughts in interaction with the world and each other. They do so on the basis of individually inherited talents and along idiosyncratic life paths, as a result of which they are still individuals. In doing so, they affect and are affected by their environment. This is the solution to the 'structure and agency' problem.

In the entrepreneurship literature, there have been studies of differences in entrepreneurship between large and small firms. There was a time, in Schumpeterian innovation studies, that small entrepreneurial firms were seen as more innovative, in 'creative destruction'. There is still some of that but now there is recognition that small and large firms both have advantages and drawbacks in innovation (Nooteboom, 1994). With small firms being generally younger and having fewer vested interests in sunk investments, they are less wary than large firms of cannibalising such investments, wanting to extend their life cycles. Being more dependent on the firm for their income, they are more motivated, willing to economise on personal spending in the (most likely) challenging period of establishing their business or developing their innovation before they have anything to show for it as security for a loan. They tend to have fewer hierarchical levels than large firms, where decision-making can be sluggish along many levels, stifling diversity and isolating top management from the markets of products and supply. A drawback of small firms is that they have fewer resources and may suffer from the diseconomies of small scale, for instance by not having access to specialist staff, for example for legal affairs, marketing or specialist technicians and scientists. Larger firms have a greater spread of risk across multiple products and markets, and more resources for research labs, distribution channels and brand advertising. A possible solution is to let small firms do the risky ventures in their early stages and hand over a newly developed innovation to a larger firm for scaling up, efficient production, distribution and marketing, in synergy with other products and backed by an established brand name.

In biotechnology, for example, firms that develop new active substances or production methods are typically small, with original and exploratory views. Larger pharmaceutical companies then conduct the testing for regulatory approval and the large-scale production and marketing of new end products, typically with a narrower (and exploitative) orientation.

Big firms sometimes try to invigorate their innovative potential by taking over an entrepreneurial small firm, but this often smothers the small firm in the bureaucracy of the larger one. A better strategy is to leave the small firm autonomous and invest in it, helping it with scaling up, legal complications, and distribution and marketing, which would also be a DC.

1.2 Criticism

In the DC literature, a distinction is made between different levels of capability (Collis, 1994; Winter, 2003): zero-order or operational capabilities, first-order capabilities of new configurations of operational capabilities, or core competencies and third-order DC. Teece, Pisano and Shuen (1997) defined DCs as the 'firm's ability to integrate, build and reconfigure internal and external competencies to address quickly changing environments'. To call DC the ability to reconfigure competencies is almost a tautology. Core competencies distinguish a firm. Teece (2007) defined the highest order DCs as 'sensing, seizing and transforming competencies that, aggregated, direct the various ordinary competencies and the second-order dynamic capabilities'. To see DC as transforming competencies is also almost a tautology. The theory of DC needs to explain how this reconfiguration and transforming of competence works.

What is the agenda? Dynamic capabilities has a variety of forms, and searching for the correct, universal definition may be counterproductive. It is not a unitary concept and requires a multilevel paradigm (Schilke *et al.*, 2018: 403). Schilke *et al.* (2018: 376) urged scholars to broaden the scope and embrace other perspectives. That is what this Element sets out to do.

The study of DC is interdisciplinary, involving different literatures beyond the SM literature. In a meta-study, Bindra *et al.* (2020) found that learning was the subject that came up most in the publications studied. In another meta-study, by Schilke *et al.* (2018), the theories most often found to be used were Resourced Based View, organisational learning, evolutionary economics and transaction cost economics (TCE). How are these perspectives connected? Concerning knowledge, clarification of the relation between individual and collective organisational knowledge (Spender, 1996a) is needed. Is knowledge a state or a process?

Treatment of organisational learning requires a theory of knowledge and truth, an underlying philosophy (epistemology) and a corresponding psychology. The theory of knowledge adopted here is interpretive and non-positivistic, as Spender (1996b) proposed. It does not entail prior deduction from existing concepts and then confrontation with observation statements, but it involves the formation of concepts from experience. One can have information that economists often call non-rival: if I give you information, I still have it. Knowledge is not static or stored away as if in a chest of drawers but a process of development that assimilates experience into cognitive frames and adapts them when the experience does not quite fit. Knowledge entails learning. It is a process of building as well as discarding. The epistemology is that of pragmatism, where truth is 'warranted assertibility', adopted from Dewey, in which part of the truth of something is whether it works in solving practical problems.

There are also DCs of collaborative relations for efficiency and innovation, and understanding this requires sociology. Dynamic capabilities are embedded in networks and managing them is also a DC, relatively neglected in the DC literature (Schilke *et al.*, 2018: 418). An exception is the work of Zheng *et al.* (2011).

Schilke *et al.* found 27 articles that indicate the need for attention to process dimensions (Schilke *et al.*, 2018: 419). Tsoukas and Chia (2002) take a process view of an organisation, as a continual process of change in interaction with its environment. Understanding processes of change requires a theory of causality, for example to distinguish the role of agents from other causal factors. In their meta-study of 298 publications, Schilke *et al.* (2018: 406) found this requirement mentioned in 28 articles. In view of the role of communication in teams, where individual and collective knowledge come together, and between collaborating firms, for learning, one might benefit even from a theory of language, in a clarification of 'sensemaking'. I agree, and add that this process view also applies to knowledge and should include, in particular, how the 'sensing, seizing and reconfiguring' Teece (2007) advocated proceeds in interaction of the firm with its environment.

2 Knowledge and Learning

2.1 Epistemology

Penrose already noted in 1959 that knowledge is key in managerial cognition, identifying new options for configuring and using resources. In Austrian economics, Kirzner (1973) spoke of entrepreneurial alertness. Yet the 'knowledge-based theory of the firm' goes back to Marshall, who saw the firm as a form of organisation that manages and develops knowledge (Foss, 2002; Loasby, 2002; Richardson, 2002). Spender (1996a) pleaded for knowledge as the focus of DC, and Spender and Grant (1996) provided an overview.

Knowledge is embedded in frames of mind, partly documented, but largely tacit. A frame of mind is triggered by the context, activating a repertoire of actions. In organisations they take the form of organisational routines (Nelson & Winter, 1982), developed in practice and in interaction between people. When tacit, the knowledge is often too rich or vague, meaning that it can be complex and variable, context-dependent and indeterminate or flexible, requiring professional judgement in its practice. Being 'locked up' in people, tacit knowledge does not easily filter through to competitors, which contributes to having a distinctive competitive advantage. However, due to staff turnover, naturally or through poaching, firms can lose the knowledge and their competitive advantage because it was not documented.

A fitting philosophy of science is American pragmatic philosophy (by scholars like Peirce, James and Dewey), which has similar views in Europe, in the 'continental' philosophies of Wittgenstein, Nietzsche and Heidegger (Malachowski, 2013). Pragmatism takes the practical working of things and their usefulness in solving practical problems as one of the criteria of their truth. This runs parallel to considerations of logic and plausibility, meaning consistency with other established knowledge, experience and facts, if those can be agreed upon. The latter qualification is made in view of a famous debate in the philosophy of science (Lakatos & Musgrave, 1970) that facts are theory-laden so that they cannot always be objectively agreed upon. However, that is often exaggerated: the theory locked in facts is often irrelevant to the difference in theory at issue.

Damasio (2003) argued that the brain makes webs of neural connections that represent, on the lowest and unconscious level, internal processes of metabolism, the flow of fluids and neural connections that regulate the body. Above the representations of bodily processes, representations are made of phenomena from outside the body, perhaps not so much unlike the old notion of association, going back to David Hume. As we go higher up in cognition, at some level there are representations of representations that somehow constitute consciousness, in some not yet understood fashion.

Gerald Edelman (1987) proposed a 'neural Darwinism': in the brain, ideas take the form of neuronal networks, where the neurons 'fire' more frequently and strongly as the corresponding ideas are 'successful' and 'work'. The neuronal networks also trigger each other's firing, and get connected, in association, when firing simultaneously. Patterns of connection may occur in competition with each other ('Darwinism'). With competition between ideas, as parallel neuronal patterns, we may be said to be in two minds about something.

Cognitive science distinguishes between declarative memory of facts, figures, names, dates, and procedural knowledge of processes. One forgets the former more easily than the latter, and embedding declarative knowledge in a process of narration may help recall. In teams, narrative is therefore important for joint memory. Narrative also makes the universality of concepts concrete.

Cognition is only partly explicit and rational, in the form of subconscious decision heuristics, as shown by psychology (Kahneman & Tversky, 1979) and behavioural economics. This has not been covered thoroughly in the DC literature (Bingham & Eisenhardt, 2011). The heuristics are not all rational, but part of subconscious framing. One heuristic is that of the loss frame, where one goes to greater lengths to prevent loss than to gain something. This appears, for example, in the later discussion of trust. This heuristic was of adaptive value in human evolution, because loss can imply death, and gain not. In choice situations now it is often irrational, for example in taking legal action that has no chance of succeeding. Another heuristic is to generalise on the basis of statistically too few observations. That has adaptive value in responding fast in threatening situations or upcoming opportunities but is also often irrational, such as in jumping to conclusions. Another heuristic is that of escalation of commitment, where past sacrifices for an effort are used as an argument to continue an effort, while it might be more rational to let bygones be bygones and rather focus on future gains and losses. Yet it has great emotional force, and can yield irrational clinging to a losing strategy, such as not withdrawing from a war zone because then so many soldiers would have died for nothing.

2.1.1 Scripts

In the analysis of organisational routines, one may use the notion of a script (Abelson, 1976; Shank & Abelson, 1977). A script is a composition of connected nodes. It can be a model of a practice, a production process, logic, theory and sentences. It has an upward causation of how the nodes constitute the script and a downward causation of how the script enables and constrains the nodes, constituting the logic of the routine. The word 'logos', translated as logic, or rationality, originally derives from a notion of composition or bringing together, from the Latin '*legein*', which means reading out, naming or collecting (*Van Dale* Dutch etymological dictionary). The script is a model of that. Scripts connect individual actions or thoughts in an organisation. Those are inserted in the nodes and develop in action in those nodes.

This is in turn connected with pragmatism and in the logic of how things fit together and work. It is also a convenient tool in the praxeology of economics, as Lachmann (1978) advocated. It is useful in innovation theory: if an innovation does not fit in the script of the user, its adoption is problematic, necessitating a change in the user script.

The script notion is applied widely, for example as the primary process of production in an organisation. It is a model of a complex adaptive system (CAS), combining different subsystems, whose actions are constrained by its place in the larger system. In a node, there are alternative ways of performing it in subscripts, as several ways of contributing to the routine. In turn, the script is a node in an overarching superscript.

The classical case of a script is that of a restaurant (Shank & Abelson, 1977), with nodes of arrival, entry, seating, choice of food, serving, eating, payment and departure. In a self-service restaurant, the order of nodes changes: arrival, food selection, payment, seating, eating and departure. This does not leave the nodes unchanged. Seating now includes carrying a tray of food to a table. Different activities can be substituted in a node, such as the various forms in the payment node: cash, credit card, debit card or smartphone. The nodes are not necessarily the same in every restaurant: for example, in the eating node, chopsticks may be used instead of knives and forks. The script as a whole fits into the node of a higher-level superscript, such as a supply chain for delivery to the restaurant, zoning regulations and parking facilities. In an organisation, a departmental subscript needs to fit into an overall organisational script.

A script is intended to be constant, a model of a routine, to be applied again and again. The knowledge about it is mostly tacit but can, to some extent, be codified in protocols and textbooks. It is, however, always incomplete with tacit underlying assumptions that are taken for granted, such as not stuffing food in your pocket in a restaurant (while doggy bags will be permitted). Each node has its own range of currently admissible subscripts, such as paying cash or submitting a card's pin code. Paying by cheque was a subscript but is now rarely used, as it has been replaced by debit or credit cards. New processes may sprout from the nodes. In the eating subscript, chopsticks may replace Western cutlery. The subscript is in turn a script, but the deeper down one gets in a hierarchy of scripts and subscripts, the more tacit and self-evident it becomes.

In the general notion of a script, beyond the organisational kind, the connections between nodes can denote a temporal, causal, logical or linguistic sequence. In an organisation, it is a model of a causal and temporal sequence of production, where one part of the whole project produces and passes a component of a product on to another part of the project to integrate it in a connected structure. Different nodes can converge, representing a shared resource. In a theory, the links can represent a chain of argument. In language, it can be a sentence, connecting nodes by grammar and syntax.

Professional practice entails using a script, but also supplementing or adjusting it, in 'tinkering' with it. Lévi-Strauss called it 'bricolage' (do it yourself) – you have to learn it or grow into it. The practice is often learned in something like a master–apprentice relation. Not everything in the practice can be specified and codified in a manual. The practice will be too rich for that, with many incompletely specifiable elements that can change from one context to another. The adjustment is not random experimentation, but it is directed to the purpose. This is discussed in the literature on communities of practice (Brown & Duguid, 1996; Burgelman, 1983). Novices have to participate in 'peripheral participation' before they become seasoned practitioners. That flies in the face of a tendency to try and specify the practice completely in a protocol, as happened in a system change for the operation of markets in hospitals and psychiatric practice. Fixed protocols of legitimate practice were needed there so that insurance companies could conduct evaluations for funding approval. This resulted from the old notion of practice as something fixed and present that could be seen as rigorous, complete and constant. Yet an organisation chart rarely represents actual lines of communication and collaboration or the improvisations needed for real practice. Such formal structures arise from a fear of chaos, a lack of confidence in flexibility, a lack of trust and the desire for reliability and control to avoid risks, which is never completely possible.

2.1.2 Causality

To understand organisational routines and scripts, one needs a theory of the causality of action that incorporates agency. That is found in the multiple causality of Aristotle:

Type of cause

- Efficient:
  Agents or forces that do things: individuals, organisations, government agencies, unions, elites, political groups, racial groups, social classes, employers, management, workers, immigrants
- Final:
  Why agents do things: goals, aims of projects, views on the good life, values, ethics, striving for power, wealth, enjoyment of art, recreation, sport, exercise, adventure, excitement, travel, economic growth, knowledge, science, preservation of nature

- Material:

  The means through which things are done: loans, wealth, natural resources, infrastructure (roads, telecommunication, airports), housing, information, communication channels
- Formal:

  How things are done: mechanisms, knowledge, skills, technology, education, habits, myths, rituals
- Conditional:

  Circumstances that affect action: markets, institutions, laws, trust, freedoms, climate, safety, viruses, geography, fashion, festivities, religion, networks, urbanisation
- Exemplary:

  Examples that are followed: images, role models, designs, diagrams

In short, in the analysis of action, it is useful to determine who the agents are, what their aims are, whether they have the requisite means for their task, the required knowledge and skills, as well as the circumstances and conditions of their work.

The conditional cause can vary. Teece (2007) mentioned regulations, technological standards, partners and other institutions. The conditional cause can enable or constrain, and it affects the other causes. It can affect the final cause, in laws, labour regulations and agreements, corruption, social habits, taboos. It can take the form of removing an obstacle. Take a waterway with a sluice. The water presses on the sluice door, and opening that door releases the water. A frozen canal provides a skating surface, while to enable gliding the pressure of the narrow iron of the skate melts the ice. The sea between Sweden and Finland can be so cold that a car can race on the ice: the weight of the car is not enough to melt the ice and make the car slide.

Aristotle made the mistake of assigning a final cause to nature, which was dealt a fatal blow by Francis Bacon. Since then, causality was conceptualised as a mechanical process, such as colliding billiard balls. Subsequently, causality came to be seen as a purely formal, consistent succession of cause and effect. In the eighteenth century, David Hume showed that regular succession does not prove a law, as there is no logical necessity of the uniformity of nature, with ongoing succession of the presumed cause and effect. To accept a regularity as law-like, one needs to set out a causal process that is plausible in the sense of aligning with what is accepted in the results of science.

An irony of the history of ideas is that economists strive for mechanical causality, in equilibria of supply and demand, while Aristotelian multiple causality, including the final cause, is eminently fit to deal with human action in the economy, with markets and institutions as conditional causes. Institutions as rules of the game are clearly part of the conditional cause. The exemplary cause provides an example that can be followed, in mimicry. The material causes may be self-made or adopted from the environment. The formal cause may be a rule or a habit, assimilated in training or practice, or may be self-constructed.

In an organisation, the exemplary cause is often a prominent leader, perhaps from the past, who forms a foundation myth, such as that of Steve Jobs, who serves as a role model to be imitated. The advantage of an exemplary cause is that it is not a command or a procedure spelled out in a manual but allows for some leeway of interpretation or emphasis, and hence creativity, which is more inspirational.

A powerful example of the exemplary cause is narrative. If you want people to follow, for example COVID-19 protocols, you can quote statistics or the findings of scholars but it is probably more effective to give a telling example of someone who failed to follow the rules and contracted the virus, with dire effects. The use of narrative connects to the importance of procedural as opposed to declarative memory.

2.2 Knowledge as a Process

Knowledge is a process of making sense of one's environment, assimilating experience in existing mind frames and accommodating them when experience fails to fit. In other words, knowledge is interpretation and adaptation. As indicated before, social psychology and behavioural economics show that thoughts and opinions are largely subconscious, and that makes it difficult to be critical by introspection. By assimilating contrary or complementary opinions, one can correct one's prejudices. This learning by interaction does not work when one is only receptive to opinions that already fit, as happens in the echo chambers of social media. It is often wise to follow others, in the 'wisdom of crowds' (Surowiecki, 2004), but that works only if members of the crowd are diverse and independent, and not swayed by others in a group to follow their views. Discussion can derail in groupthink, where dissent is suppressed, even unawares, by authority, charisma of some vocal participant and pressure to achieve consensus (Solomon, 2006). Bubbles arise, in stock markets and fashion, when people think they know what others do or think and anticipate developments accordingly. There may be 'information cascades' where people sequentially herd together, following some misinformed first movers (Surowiecki, 2004).

Life is full of coordination challenges which we brilliantly solve by subconsciously anticipating what others will do, such as when we walk on a sidewalk or drive in traffic. This anticipation is generally based on shared habits, institutions or culture.

The question is how learning takes place and how knowledge develops. There is learning by absorbing existing knowledge, often tacitly adopted by participation and repetition in practice, in routines (Nelson & Winter, 1982), and there is learning by experimentation, which can lead to discovery (Teece & Pisano, 1994). Learning by study has been called deliberate versus emergent learning (Mintzberg & Waters, 1985). Similarly, Zollo and Winter (2002) discussed deliberate as opposed to experiential learning. Yet deliberate learning also depends on experience. Deliberately reading a book is assimilation, like participating in a script.

Aristotle already argued for a form of development: in 'entelechy', development of form arises from the realisation of potential. An example is the oak that grows from the acorn. We now have the concept of DNA that generates bodily forms. Is there something like organisational DNA? The next question is to what extent and how the realisation of potential can generate the emergence of new potential, in what the philosopher Schelling called 'potentialisation'.

Nelson and Winter (1982) distinguished between operational and search routines but did not clarify how those work. A distinction has been made between single-loop learning, in learning adjustments to operational routines from practical experience, and more fundamental double-loop learning in the change of underlying assumptions (Argyris & Schön, 1994). The latter is relatively scarce. Apart from assumptions that can be changed, even if they are ingrained, there are inevitably fundamental, tacit, background assumptions and ideologies that cannot and often need not be specified and that one is not even aware of. An example is the notion of causality.

March (1991) distinguished between exploitation, in the effective and efficient use of existing resources, with some incremental innovation, and exploration, in the development of new resources and capabilities, in radical innovation. The challenge is to specify how, by what process or logic one does exploitation, for survival in the short term, as well as exploration, for survival in the long term. Burchhardt Marcussen claims that this has not yet been achieved in the DC literature.

Teece (2007) characterised dynamic capabilities as 'not allocating means to ends, [but] discover[ing] and create[ing] new ends and means'. Dynamic capabilities are said to entail scanning, sensemaking and decision-making. Narayaman *et al.* (2011) proposed that they include rational inference of cause–effect relations, rules for experimentation and the ability to utilise organisational memory. They also include exchanging codified knowledge with others. These proposals are largely tautological labels on our ignorance. What do alertness of entrepreneurs (Kirzner) and scanning (Teece) mean? Dynamic capability entails 'discovery of new ends and means'. Opportunities that an entrepreneur finds while scanning are discussed as if they are already lying somewhere, ready to be discovered.

How does all that work? The question is to what extent, and how, organisations can develop dynamic capabilities to escape from inertia. How is it a process?

In what sense and to what extent is this search blind? How is it related to evolutionary selection and to what extent can it anticipate survival in selection? Teece (2007) recognises that opportunities are not found but made. How is that done? On page 1323 he states: 'One must accumulate and then filter information from professional and social contacts to create a conjecture or a hypothesis about the likely evolution of technologies, customer needs, and marketplace responses'. That is still fairly vague.

Lavie (2006) indicated the following elements in capability reconfiguration: substitution, evolution, transformation and an intermediate mode in which some routines are modified, and others are discarded. That sounds promising but remains unspecified. I think such processes need to be accompanied by experimentation, interaction with the environment of markets and institutions, between internal and external capabilities and conditions. Teece and others recognise that customers and suppliers can offer ideas for innovation, in what they call open innovation (Chesbrough, 2003). However, they seem to assume that there is first the sensing and subsequently the seizing of an opportunity as if it already exists. I propose that sensing and shaping an opportunity occurs in trying things out and utilising success as an ingredient for further development.

Established resource configurations and capabilities can become an obstacle to innovation (Leonard-Barton, 1992). Crossan and Berdrow (2003: 534) noted that 'It is difficult to change institutionalized learning prevalent at the organizational level'. In learning, one must therefore also unlearn. To accomplish that, one needs insight about what to let go, as well as motivation and the need to do so. The philosopher Hegel proposed that we get to know something in its limits and failures. For that, we need to apply what we have in new environments. In evolutionary terms: we must submit it to new selection environments. That is not only needed to find the limits of validity of what we have, but also to explore opportunities for renewal, in the new environment, inspired by what turns out to work where our own practice fails. That, I propose, is the crux of experimental learning.

2.2.1 Cycle of Discovery

A theory of learning is Nooteboom's (2000) Cycle of Discovery (COD), inspired by the work of Jean Piaget.[1] The theory claims to apply to individuals

---

[1] See Flavell (1967) and Piaget (1970). Piaget's work goes back to the 1930s to 1950s and has met with considerable criticism. This has led to his experiments being replicated and extended in

as well as organisations. It has largely been ignored in the DC literature. The underlying theory of cognition is that it develops from *assimilating* experience into existing ideas (frames) and *accommodating* them, adapting cognitive frames or developing new ones, when this fails. This opens up the black box from the DC literature of scanning opportunities. It can be both deliberate and accidental. It shows a process of how learning arises from experimentation, in interaction with the environment.

The basic premise is that new ideas arise by applying an old idea in new settings, where they are confronted with conditions in which they do not fully fit, raising a challenge to their survival. For that, established practice is *generalised*, meaning that it is brought into new environments where it meets new challenges of survival. There is a link to evolutionary theory in that generalisation is a step into a new selection environment. To survive, the product or idea has to adapt. This can take the form of retrying options that formerly failed, which requires organisational memory, in documents or from the experience of older staff. This leaves the basic structure or *architecture* (Henderson & Clark, 1990) of the practice the same, while varying the choice of elements in the architecture of existing activities, in *differentiation*. When that is not adequate, the next step is to incorporate elements from a local practice that is successful where one's own is not into the existing architecture, perhaps adopting entire local practices, called *reciprocation*. This sounds like an elaboration of Lavie's notion of substitution and yields hybrids of old and new elements. This is akin to the logic of metaphor: one learns to see something different and new in the light of something familiar.

This amalgamation of old and new elements into an old basic design or logic yields hybrids – a familiar phenomenon in the history of innovation (Mokyr, 1990). The stage of *hybridisation* is important for exploring the potential of foreign elements without making the sacrifice of dumping existing basic logic or design yet. This stage allows one to explore where the problems lie in the integration of old and new. It also indicates which aspects of the existing structure limit the full utilisation of new potential and create bottlenecks and inefficiencies. This provides hints about the direction for promising more structural change, in double-loop learning.

This may lead to the next stage, where one experiments with more structural change, in *accommodation*, in different configurations or architectures of old and reconfigured or new elements, to reinstitute order (a new order) in a new

---

different ways, some of which confirmed his claims while others contradicted them. His thinking has become controversial but overall it still stands and remains included in modern textbooks of developmental psychology (Leman et al., 2019). The crux in this text is the notion that cognition develops from action, in assimilation and accommodation, which does not seem to be contested.

structure. This may be an elaboration of Lavie's transformation. This is a concretisation of the unlearning mentioned before.

When a new basic design emerges, it is initially far from perfect, may not yet realise its full potential and may for a long time carry along residuals from the old logic that hamper efficiency and need to be ferreted out for a full breakthrough of the novelty, in *consolidation*. Accommodation and consolidation may be an elaboration of Crossan and Berdrow's (2003) notion of integrating and institutionalising. Next, the new standard may be differentiated to cater to different market segments, in product differentiation.

The paintings of J. M. W. Turner show the parallel existence of new, somewhat lumbering steamboats and elegant old sailing ships. In the transition from building wooden bridges to the use of iron, at first the old constructive principle of swallow tails to connect wooden parts was maintained, while with iron there is the alternative of welding. In an analysis of artillery practice, it was found that when a cannon was fired, a soldier backed up a few steps (more than needed) to protect himself from the recoil. Why? The conclusion was that this was a leftover from old-time horse-drawn artillery, where at firing someone had to step back to hold the horses in their fright at the explosion.

The breakthrough of a novel design is gradual but fast, relative to the long process of transferring the old product or idea to a new field, making minor adjustments, creating hybrids and tinkering with attempts at structural change.

The cycle of discovery shows how transformation is not ongoing flux but requires the alternation of stability and change in the relative stability of assimilation and the radical change of accommodation. One needs time to discover the limits of validity of the old and to experiment with variations and shifts. There is much trial and error but also inference of possibilities for adaptation. The cycle of discovery alternates between exploitation and exploration (March, 1991): differentiation and reciprocation are incremental and exploitative, but prepare for the exploration of accommodation, consolidation, product differentiation and exploitation again.

The logic of discovery explains why innovation through collaboration between individuals is effective. Having to explain one's knowledge and practice to a partner entails a step of generalisation into the thoughts of the other, from where one obtains new insights into the limits of one's views and practice. This yields a need to adjust; first on the basis of reframing it using previous experience, and if that does not work, partners in collaboration offer each other ideas, in reciprocation, in an exchange of novel elements to try out, and in exchanging design principles in search of solving the constraints and problems that arise from the resulting hybrids. It is much easier to have a partner with a different but experienced view to stimulate and assist the process than having to do everything by one's own inference.

This may contribute to a deeper understanding of the familiar notion of absorptive capacity (Cohen & Levinthal, 1990): having more experience, one is better able to reframe, in cognition and competence, what a partner offers in the process of reciprocation. The other side of the coin of learning by interaction is rhetorical ability – the ability to help a partner absorb what one offers, notably by the use of apt metaphors. The more experience one has, the greater the fund of one's metaphors. That is also a DC.

The script notion can be used to further elaborate the cycle of discovery. In differentiation, more than the usual subscripts are substituted into the node, tapping from previous experience, stored in individual memories or archives. In reciprocation, subscripts or entire nodes are taken from outside scripts into the new environment. In accommodation, the structure of nodes in the script is changed, with old and new nodes. In consolidation, redundant or inconsistent subscripts or nodes are eliminated, such as waiters in a self-service restaurant. One may, however, need security agents and attendants to clear the dishes.

The notion of a script may help in strategic marketing. If an innovation of a product or service does not fit into a user's script it is difficult for them to adopt and the innovation is likely to fail, unless a new script is provided along with the product.

2.2.2 Entrepreneurship

The cycle of discovery is recognisable in the practice of firms innovating by internationalisation. While internationalisation used to be primarily a strategy to maintain growth after home market saturation, it set in motion a process of discovery. Companies started to identify and understand it as such and subsequently employed it as a deliberate strategy of innovation. This mode of operation was confirmed in a conversation with a former chief executive officer of Shell: they originally engaged in internationalisation only to increase sales until they discovered that this yields innovation, after which they adopted it as a deliberate strategy. This illustrates how the process can require strategic change, from market expansion utilising economy of scale to allowing for divergence for the sake of innovation.

From the cycle of discovery one can deduce several forms of entrepreneurship or DC. One can maintain existing capabilities and change the way in which they are applied and governed in interaction with the new context, or one can change the capabilities. In the stage of taking a practice into a new environment, in generalisation, there is a widening of orientation – not yet on the competence side but on the governance side – of opening up to new institutions and environmental culture. In the stage of differentiation, one relaxes organisational focus to allow for the renewed try-out of old practices. In reciprocation, the opening up is more on the competence side, of trying out elements from outside, local practices, in hybridisation. In accommodation, the departure from the old focus is more radical, allowing for structural change in basic architecture. Consolidation is more incremental, and the focus narrows again, directed at increasing efficiency, and then there is differentiation of the product to optimise market fit.

A variation on the logic is not to move into a new environment but to invite a variety of views from other environments. This is related to the subject of 'the wisdom of crowds', which I discussed before. Such novelty might benefit from the admission or invitation of outside practices.

If everything changes, can change change? The principle that to change something – a theory, a practice, a product – one way to carry it into a new environment seems valid, but other logics of change may exist or emerge in further research.

Another way to innovate is not to transfer an existing practice to a new context but to start a new product next to the existing one. There, variety of ideas, speed and efficiency are enhanced by collaborating with a partner who already has the assets and experience. This requires a DC of setting up and governing alliances that I will discuss later.

2.2.3 Language

In the interactive development of knowledge, communication is key. The DC literature mentions sensemaking. What is that and how does it work? To understand learning, one must have a theory of meaning and its change. From the theory of language, one may use the distinction that the philosopher Frege made between, 'reference and sense', (Thiel, 1965). Reference is what an expression refers to (the cat on the mat), while sense is the way in which something is identified as such (fur, purring, soft paws, sharp nails, mouse catching). For a proposition, reference is its truth value. One development of the meaning of sensemaking as mentioned in the DC literature is learning how one identifies things or truths. Reference is public and shared, while sense is individual and grows from personal experience.

The meaning of a word depends on context. In understanding meaning in a sentence one can see the sentence as a script, with words as nodes; in 'downward causation' the sentence (script) limits which potential meanings of the word (node) are admissible and can work. That does not necessarily leave such admissible sense unaffected. The sentence and its action context may clarify or tweak the meaning of a word. A story about someone sitting at a desk may show that the chair has no backrest. That is unusual, but it can make sense and may then be added to the repertoire of the sense of desk chair. I have seen a picture in a newspaper of someone sitting in a stuffed cow for a chair. Even the stuffed cow may henceforth be part of the connotation, the sense, of chair.

Ferdinand de Saussure (1979) distinguished between the intersubjective order of language at any moment ('langue'), such as the established lingo and rhetoric in a team or firm, rules of grammar and syntax as well as canonical meanings on the one hand, and the movement of living language use in time ('parole') on the other hand. The two are needed for the combination of mutual understanding in a firm and personal creativity. To combine the two, even poetry might be a good exercise. The public, intersubjective, collective order ('langue') may be captured up to a point in documents. 'Parole' is personal and gives variety to language, but also needs to align with 'langue' to enable communication and mutual understanding. 'Langue' is language on the level of the script, with 'parole' being on the level of the subscript. 'Parole' is needed to bring in creativity, based on personal experience, which may shift 'langue' a bit. This helps to analyse the relation between individual and collective, socially shared knowledge, and complements the notions of sense and reference. Sense is personal, associated with parole, in basing reference on personal experience. To arrive at shared reference, which is needed for collaboration, it needs to connect with the 'langue' in use.

3 Organisation as an Entity

3.1 Cognitive Distance

As people develop their cognition on the basis of individually inherited talents and personal life paths, they differ in their knowledge and capabilities. This *cognitive distance* (CD) presents a challenge as well as an opportunity. The opportunity is that variety of cognition is a source of innovation, in crafting Schumpeterian novel combinations. The challenge is that with CD it is more difficult to understand each other and to collaborate and utilise opportunities from cognitive variety.

In this context, cognition is a wide concept, including variation in intellectual knowledge as well as differences in motivation and morality of how people should deal with each other. CD creates barriers to mutual understanding, due to limited *absorptive capacity* (Cohen & Levinthal, 1990), as well as wider challenges of collaboration, including mismatched moral and motivational aspects, often due to cultural differences. In other words, distance includes issues of both competence and governance. This can be compared with Herbert Simon's distinction between substantive and procedural rationality.

Optimal collaboration requires a trade-off between the upside and downside of cognitive distance, seeking optimal cognitive distance (Nooteboom, 2000; Nooteboom *et al.*, 2007), large enough to offer variety for innovation and small enough to enable collaboration. Problems arise especially when there are cultural differences, particularly between more individualistic and more collectivist countries/regions/groups. There are complications due to language differences and also stereotyping; there are differences in habits concerning openness, politeness, sincerity, formality or body language. Experience in dealing with others who think differently helps greatly, as well as conversational skills; for example the use of metaphor, accumulated knowledge, altruism, empathy and sensitivity. The distance can generate misunderstanding as well as mistrust. Trust is discussed more extensively later.

The proposition of optimal cognitive distance was tested and confirmed with an econometric model of innovation by collaboration by Nooteboom *et al.* (2007). A proxy for cognitive distance was technological distance, measured as the difference between technological profiles composed from differences in the incidence of patents in different patent classes. In the innovation literature, it is customary to recognise that patents do not necessarily yield success in profiting from innovation (Griliches, 1990). They are sometimes used not to exploit but to shield off innovation by others. However, patents are one of the few available sources of data and can be used for the present purpose as an indicator of technological distance. They may not be good indicators of innovative potential, but differences in classes of patents are reasonable indicators of technological distance.

The model included the refinement that for radical innovation cognitive distance needs to be relatively large, offering the cognitive diversity needed for Schumpeterian 'novel combinations', and in incremental innovation needs to be relatively small, avoiding inefficiencies due to misunderstanding. In the words of March (1991), exploration requires relatively large distance, while exploitation requires relatively small distance. Yet all organisations need some internal proximity, compared to the distances between firms exhibited in markets and industries As Friedrich Hayek (1945) argued, the market is characterised by dispersed and differentiated local knowledge that makes competition a discovery process. The model confirmed the hypothesis that for exploration optimal distance is larger than in exploitation: one needs to employ knowledge or competence at a larger cognitive distance. Exploratory innovations were measured as the number of patents outside the patent classes firms had before the innovation.

Cognitive distance is bridged with the aid of absorptive capacity (Cohen & Levinthal, 1990): the ability to understand and cope with differences in knowledge and skill, including morality. This depends on cumulative knowledge and experience with people who think differently. Next to absorptive capacity there is rhetorical ability – the ability to make oneself understood and help a partner to cross cognitive distance. The use of metaphor helps to explain unfamiliar things in terms that are familiar to the partner. In the model, absorptive capacity was measured as the number of patents accumulated in a certain period. A shortcoming is that it does not include the social dimension of moral distance, which might be measured by experience in collaborating with people who think differently.

An unexpected outcome of the model was that with a higher absorptive capacity due to accumulated knowledge, optimal cognitive distance increased, as expected, but the marginal increase of novelty potential with distance decreased, so that one has to search at a larger distance to find something new. Geniuses are lonely and need to go to exotic places to still catch something new. In other words, accumulating knowledge has both increasing returns in absorptive capacity and decreasing returns in novelty.

3.2 Organisational Focus

Where does knowledge reside and develop in an organisation? Next to documents and procedures, knowledge is mostly in the minds of people – in mindframes, skills and scripts. Some coherence in shared knowledge and scripts, some limitation of cognitive distance is needed to achieve a purpose. This requires coordination. How is that achieved? Witt (2005) offered a view of entrepreneurs and managers as providing cognitive leadership. This is similar to Penrose's managerial cognition, but personnel other than managers also contribute. How does it all come together? A certain degree of joint cognitive and motivational orientation of personnel is needed for an organisation to function more or less efficiently. Focus is needed to not let knowledge go off in all directions and to reduce the need to negotiate goals of action and terms of collaboration at every instant.

In the literature, organisation has been seen as a system for sensemaking (Weick, 1995), collective mind (Weick & Roberts, 1993), system of shared meanings (Smircich, 1983). McKelvey (1982) proposed that organisations are characterised by dominant competencies. Nelson and Winter (1982) used the term 'routines', but it brings some ambiguity and confusion, therefore I prefer McKelvey's terminology. What, precisely, are all these?

In earlier work (Nooteboom, 2000; 2006; 2009), I proposed that organisations require an organisational focus in order to exploit resources effectively. Here I propose that such focus yields an organisational identity that has some stability. Organisational focus enables but also constrains absorption of novelty that feeds organisational change. It functions as a filter for admitting and accepting outside ideas. In other words, organisations are indeed subject to greater or lesser inertia (Hannan & Freeman, 1984). It remains to be seen to what extent organisations may escape inertia, which is needed for radical innovation or double-loop learning.

Organisational focus is a device for integrating knowledge in organisations and selecting external knowledge. It also has a function of staff selection as well as adaptation. It selects people in recruitment, which often results from self-selection of personnel joining the organisation because they feel affinity with it, plus adaptation, in socialisation into the firm and training incoming personnel.

Cognitive activities in an organisation require some embodiment to crystallise, direct and stabilise cognition and communication. For the internal function of coordination, we find the exemplary behaviour of organisational heroes, often a founder and/or, corresponding myths and rituals. More formalised forms of organisation include procedures for reporting, decision-making, recruitment, contracting, intellectual property and the like.

To facilitate these and other functions, focus must be embodied in some visible form, such as in symbols, logos, advertising style and external communication. These visible forms serve as signalling devices to outsiders. That is needed for recognition and identification by other stakeholders, such as customers and suppliers, and as a basis of the (self-)selection process of incoming staff. Organisations develop their own specialised semiotic systems, in language, symbols, role models, metaphors, myths and rituals. The focus of an organisation includes several fundamental assumptions: consideration of the human being and its environment, whether the human being is more self-centred or altruistic, whether risk is seen as a threat or opportunity, and whether the world is considered to be mastered or submitted to, is predictable or uncertain and if nature is to be exploited or saved (Weick, 1995). This is organisational culture. It differs between organisations to the extent that they have different goals and have accumulated different experiences, in different industries, technologies, markets and cultures. The central difference between firm and market is that in the former such focus is made and in the latter it is not, or to a much lesser extent (there is still a remaining, shared cognitive focus from a common industrial and market structure, and national or regional culture), or to some extent in forms of collaboration with some shared understanding. The market therefore has the higher *potentiality* of variety of performance, and the firm has the higher *actuality* of performance.

Organisations or parts of it that are orientated at efficient production or exploitation will have a narrow focus, and organisations orientated at innovation a wider one. Among other things, organisational distance entails difference in the width and content of the focus. Cognitive proximity need not, however, be the same across the whole organisation. There can be pockets of corporate entrepreneurship, in marketing or research departments, with relatively large internal cognitive distance, or wide focus, larger innovative potential, but still smaller than the variety present in a market of independent firms yet yielding the advantage of some resources with economies of scale in the larger firm.

The classic case of the use of outside cognition is the 'wisdom of crowds'. A paradigm example is that of people guessing the weight of a cow on show in a fair (Surowiecki, 2004). Taking the average of all guesses gives a pretty good approximation and shows that guesses are often better than those of people who are thought to be in the know.

A different case is that of the Linux software system as an open-source community that benefits from the variety of expertise and experience of the users in debugging the system. However, not all proposals for improvement are equally relevant and well-informed, and need to be vetted by a small group around the founder, Linus Thorvalds. Organisational focus is needed, not only to bring some coherence in the development of actions and ideas of personnel but also to vet what they propose and do. In a firm, the vetting is presumably (or usually) done by the board of directors. The difficulty is to maintain focus without suppressing innovative dissent and criticism.

Sharing and developing knowledge in groups, in brainstorming, may result in 'groupthink', where people do not venture deviant ideas, keeping them from thinking out of the box. Occasional seclusion may be needed, but this is to be followed by meetings to iron out discrepancies and prejudices. The appropriate tightness of focus depends on how far one wants to go with this variety. It depends on the industry, the strategic choice of exploration or exploitation, the technology involved, the freedom or constraints in the environment, the ethics adhered to and the view on what is the good life. The wider focus allows for more idiosyncrasy and diversity in cognitive distance.

It sounds paradoxical that a judgement from a diverse crowd should be evaluated and vetted by a small group of directors or an evaluation committee. The solution is that such a group should not give a substantial judgement and should only judge if the proposals or judgements from the crowd are relevant and when procedural conditions have been met, concerning diversity, independence and informedness of crowd members. This is not foolproof because judgements of relevance and informedness may still be biased. The vetting should not be substantive – judging the content of proposals, which would seem to diminish valuable diversity – but should select proposals that are not feasible in the present system. Such radical proposals might of course be the most interesting but could be reserved for future consideration.

Surowiecki (2004: 80) recounts the (rejected) proposal of the policy analysis market to open up assessment of an option in the evaluation of national security issues to voting by the public. Perhaps a firm could open up to voting on the fit of a strategic option in the organisational focus, or a shift of the focus, by loyal and trusted customers and suppliers. One could even envisage, for an environmentally responsible strategy, opening up to a wider public of citizens and administrators, but then it becomes a public institution without the guidance of the firm's focus.

To avoid suppressing diversity in groupthink or vetting and selection, one may need to have several parallel and/or competing teams, similar to the neural Darwinism in the brain, according to Edelman (1987), discussed before. One might think of parallel teams as different members of an alliance, but they would not have a shared focus and might then be working at cross purposes. Some shared focus in the alliance would be needed. Another option to break through groupthink and attachment to established views is to submit the team to the shock of a new, foreign environment. That arose in the stage of generalisation in the cycle of discovery discussed before. The openness to diverse suggestions from outside may be seen as introducing diverse environments.

One may expect that there is some typology of focus, similar perhaps to the Big Five personality traits discussed in psychology (Digman, 1990). In designing a typology that maps onto those, one might arrive at the following:

1. The extraverted firm: high on exploration, entrepreneurial, engaging in generalisation, reciprocation and accommodation, in the cycle of discovery
2. The careful firm: vigilance to threats, taking safety measures, engaging in consolidation (neuroticism in the original)
3. The solid firm: contingency planning, long term view, social and environmental policy
4. The creative firm: open to new ideas, engaging in accommodation (openness/intelligence in the original)
5. The relational firm: good in alliances, collaboration, high on trust, engaging in reciprocation (agreeableness in the original)

As in the personality field, these types all have benefits and costs (Digman, 1990; Nettle, 2006). In the DC field there is a bias of preference for the extraverted/creative firm. However, the desirability of the types depends on environmental conditions, such as degree and type of competition, local and global political and institutional conditions, the pandemic and culture and its change (Nettle, 2006).

Is there something like a psychopathic firm, a perversion of the extraverted firm, and the opposite to the solid/relational firm? It exists, for example, in the Mafia. One may speculate about the church, as being solid and relational but perhaps also introverted and overly careful.

A crucial implication of organisational focus is that by definition it yields myopia, by which the organisation may miss vital threats and opportunities. To compensate for this, one needs external partners with a different, complementary perspective. Organisational theory must therefore, at the same time, yield a theory of relations, where relations necessitate their own capabilities. There is a large literature on how to manage interfirm relations and I will discuss some of it, concerning their governance, later.

3.3 Networks

Networks are a structural feature of external relations. In addition, or in elaboration of the positioning in an external field of competitive forces, as in Porter's five forces model, modern positioning also concerns the choice, positioning and building of networks of suppliers, customers, partners in development, competitors and government agencies, in setting standards. The relevant literature is extensive and recognises structural and positional effects. Structural effects are the strength of ties, density of ties (the extent to which nodes are connected) and structural holes (the condition of a few or no connections between groups of nodes). Crossing structural holes and connecting previously unconnected groups can yield novel combinations that cross cognitive distance but can also yield opportunities for playing off parts of the network against each other (Simmel, 1950; Krackhardt, 1999; Nooteboom, 2006).

Between conflicting firms or regions at too large a cognitive distance, such a position of intermediary or boundary spanner can be difficult (Krackhardt, 1999). One can be confronted with different perspectives that are difficult to align. Crossing cultural distance can produce mistrust by one's 'home group', a loss of respect and acceptance, in suspicions of being a defector or even a traitor in catering to foreign views. This can apply in connecting otherwise unconnected regions or nations.

In the network literature, there has been a debate on the strengths of weak (Granovetter, 1973) and strong (Coleman, 1988) ties between individuals or organisations. The strength of a tie has several dimensions: frequency of interaction, duration, multiplicity (number of features included in the tie, such as finance, labour, materials, instruments, knowledge or advice), trust and specific investments. As discussed, specific investments have value only within the relationship and are lost or worth less when the relationship breaks. They often need to be made when the relationship is aimed at the novel combinations of innovation. This specificity makes parties dependent and vulnerable to power play, and specific investments will be made only when the relationship is expected to be sufficiently durable to recoup the investment. While strong ties have benefits of trust, they may generate loss of diversity, cognitive distance and flexibility.

Structural features of a network are its density – the extent to which the nodes are connected, directly or indirectly. For an optimal arrangement one can think of a combination: strong internal, local ties for governance and trust, and weak external ties, outside the firm or region, with larger cognitive distance in knowledge and competence, for the sake of diversity and innovation (Nooteboom, 2004). Variety can also be enhanced by personnel turnover, bringing in fresh ideas.

Positional features of a network are centrality, one kind of which is degree centrality, referring to the number of direct ties of a node to others in the network. This is subject to the 'Matthew effect', according to which the rich get richer: having many contacts makes one attractive for other nodes to connect to. Having many contacts can however also yield a disadvantage of being constrained in having to compromise between many conflicting interests. Another positional feature is 'betweenness centrality', which is the extent to which paths of connection in the network pass through the node, as a hub or a crossroads. This has advantages of collecting knowledge from distant sources. However, it requires sufficient absorptive capacity to profit from the diversity of throughcoming perspectives, which can lead to cognitive overload.

A region or an organisation can aspire to be a hub, with high degree centrality, with many direct links or with betweenness centrality. The hub can be a destination, such as a tourist or conference centre, a monument or an international centre in some activity, such as the International Court of Justice in The Hague or the World Health Organization in Geneva. The hub can also be a transit port instead of a destination, such as an airline hub or Paris as a point you have to pass to reach other parts of France. A hub is vulnerable to policies for fighting something like COVID-19, due to travel restrictions, unless the movement or connections are virtual and online, via search engines or websites.

The network effects interact with the effects of cognitive distance (Gilsing *et al.*, 2008). Small internal cognitive distance and a lack of internal diversity may be compensated by a dense network and a high extent of degree or betweenness centrality.

The ability to master these effects of networks is also a dynamic capability.

3.4 Entropy

An organism, organisation, region and country are all examples of complex adaptive systems. Those are systems constructed from elements or subsystems, such as neutrons, protons and electrons composing atoms, atoms composing molecules, molecules composing organs, organs composing bodies, bees composing colonies, people composing organisations, firms, consumers and institutions composing markets, people and institutions composing regions or nations, nations composing supranational entities like the European Union. In emergence, the whole grows properties that the elements do not have. The elements often come together in self-organisation. The elements and the system as a whole interact with each other and with the environment of the system, resisting the rise of entropy.

Entropy can assist in understanding organisations' structure and diversity (Testa & Kier, 2000; Janow, 2003). There is even an entropy journal. Entropy is the number of alternative compositions of components that a system with given properties can have. If the properties are few or indiscriminate, entropy is large. The mathematical formula for entropy E of a system of n elements i of probability pi is $I = -\sum_i pi.\log pi$ For a system of two units of equal probability 1/2, E = 1, called a 'bit'. For a system of four elements of equal probability, E = 2 or two bits. For a system with eight elements of equal probability E = 3, or three bits. For a system with n states of equal probability, E = log$n$. A computational advantage of the log function is that log1/n = minus log$n$. E increases with the number of elements n and with their evenness, equality of pi, which is their probability of occurrence or prominence, weight or legitimacy. The effect of the number of elements is illustrated above, with n going from two to eight elements. The decrease of E with the unevenness of pi is as follows: for the case with three elements n with equal pi = 1/3, E = 1.58 and with p1 = 2/4, p2 = 1/4, p3 = 1/4, E = 1.5.

Theil (1967) used entropy as a measure of concentration of sales in markets or production in industries. Concentration is associated with a lack of variety. Pi here is the share of seller or producer i. If there is only one seller or producer, there is maximum concentration, E = 1, meaning the least entropy. The function log$n$ increases less than proportionally with n: it increases at a decreasing rate, its derivative being 1/n. This entails that the increase of entropy slows down. As disorder increases, the resistance to further increase increases. Further increase of evenness then becomes more difficult.

A puzzle concerning entropy can be seen in complex adaptive systems such as organisms and organisations. On the one hand, CASs produce order, organisation ('complexity') and in that sense decrease entropy. On the other hand, in their development they involve more units, constitute new agglomerations and new functions, and thereby increase entropy. How can that be? It depends on their heterogeneity and on the complementarity of the parts. While the subsystems integrate into a new order, they lose autonomy. To create the unity or coherence of the higher system with its new functions, the subsystems are constrained in their operation, become specialised, losing some functions or narrowing their range, and that constitutes less entropy. In a bee colony, bees are highly specialised as food seekers, gatekeepers, soldiers or feeders of the queen bee (Testa & Kier, 2000).

It is a puzzling process whereby entropy decreases by first ostensibly increasing, with more chaos and a larger number of elements, and then decreases by an increase of their unevenness, variety, yielding coherence, in a new order, and scrapping what is redundant or not valid, in that order. This is illustrated by science, with a peculiar combination of competition and collaboration between scientists. They collaborate by picking up and combining each other's diverse ideas in novel combinations and often in teams, and then eliminating attempts of other combinations that fail, and compete in doing that (Surowiecki, 2004: 166). That is how they gather reputation and build careers. Unfortunately, new work often gets ignored if it does not come from reputed, established members of the community.

Could this be mimicked in a firm? One condition is that people should be motivated not to keep knowledge to themselves, in competition with others in the community, perhaps stimulated by collective rather than individual rewards. They should be motivated to share their ideas, collaborate in teams and then scrap what misfires. This issue resembles the old problem of what to outsource and what to do inhouse. More outsourcing yields more diversity, but also increases the transaction costs of search, evaluation, agreement, specific investments, control and haggling. Organisational focus should be designed in a trade-off between diversity and transaction costs.

The formula of entropy is incomplete. One should not only consider the number, unevenness and diversity of units, but also their relations. It is through internal and external relations that identity is constituted, and order is created. If relations break down, it is a feature of decay and increasing entropy. An incoherent bunch of disconnected entities has more entropy than complementary, interacting ones. In their present breakdown of communities, in society, with dissociated individuals, entropy is increasing.

The formula for entropy could be extended as follows: $E = -\sum_{i=1}^{n} pi$, $logpi + |1 - C/M|$, where C is the number of direct connections between units, and M is its optimum, and the vertical slashes indicate absolute value. What is optimal connection depends on the purpose of the system. The maximum number of connections is $n(n\text{-}1)/2$. That is not necessarily optimal, as in an organisation where all people, or all firms in a region, connect with all, there is noise that distracts from work, and a risk of groupthink. Teams can get too large. If C = M, meaning that the number of connections is at its optimum, the addition to entropy is 0. If C = 0, if there are no connections, the addition is 1. If the number of connections is lower or higher than the optimum, there is addition to entropy. One can picture this as an $n \times n$ matrix with n units along both axes, and a surface above the matrix that represents the value of interaction for each pair of units. It is likely to have a bulge at the optimum; some connections have more value than others.

In the literature on freedom, Isaiah Berlin distinguished negative freedom, in the absence of external constraint, from positive freedom in access to resources. Here, in the CAS, the subsystems lose negative freedom in constraints imposed or accepted for fitting in the higher system but gains positive freedom in access to new functions offered by the higher-level system. There is loss of one freedom and gain of the other. This can also be applied to regions. When coherence is lacking, one can fail to realise the potential of variety, and when coherence is too tight, one immobilises the system. A region should search for the right mix of negative entropy of focus and positive entropy of diversity.

4 Organisation as a Process

4.1 Innovation

Organisations consist of many entities, concrete and abstract, such as people, with their knowledge and competencies, physical assets, documents, scripts, organisational focus, reputation, external contacts and position in networks. These serve as bases for processes of action, such as production, co-ordination, marketing and innovation. They are largely processes themselves and all adapt to contingencies.

Innovation can be incremental or radical, single-loop or double-loop. This sounds more discontinuous than it is. It is an ongoing process with an alternation of stability and change, as set out before in the cycle of discovery (COD). People develop their knowledge by assimilation and accommodation, and scripts are adapted by new substitutions in nodes, such as when payment cheques are replaced by cards and then by smartphones. New materials are introduced in production scripts. People replace each other, bringing different styles of what appear to be similar things, within the boundaries the script imposes. It is not clear whether such adaptation is to be called incremental innovation. In more radical innovation, according to the COD nodes of outside scripts or entire scripts may be adopted in reciprocation, but this is still not radical in that the architecture of the script remains the same. Changes of architecture may be more or less radical. It can be only a different sequence of existing scripts, such as the order of steps of production, or an entire reconfiguration, as in the transition to just-in-time production. For an example of minor structural change, consider Adam Smith's famous example of a pin factory. One can sharpen the pin before polishing it, but there may be reasons for turning that around. In the case of the restaurant script, if one selects food before seating, it entails a shift to self-service, which has repercussions throughout the script.

For an organisation, the developmental stage of generalisation is bringing a product into a new market, submitting it to new demands. The developmental stage of reciprocation serves to try out change to adapt to those demands. In this context, power can have an adverse effect, and Child (2002) demonstrated it in a study of international joint ventures in China. American multi-nationals had much power in the technology and employment they offered, and access to their home market, by which they could force local partners to adopt their scripts, lessening the need for their adaptation. Less powerful European firms had to accommodate more to local practice, which served as a source of innovation, so that in the longer run they won out. They adapted, in part, to Chinese personnel policies, use of technology, deliberative networks ('quanxi'), governmental relations and their use in access to markets.

Organisations are complex adaptive systems, where subsystems are fitted into a larger system, yielding higher functions, in which the subsystems must surrender some of their scope of functioning, for the sake of systemic coherence. That is the function of organisational focus.

In an emerging literature, that coherence of a CAS is modelled with the notion of entropy. There, every organism is in danger of falling into the disorder of increasing entropy, when left to itself. To prevent that, it must interact with its environment to absorb 'food' and shed 'waste'. For an organisation that is the reciprocation with outside scripts, turnover of personnel, to absorb novel ideas and to drop disfunctional scripts, shown up by this reciprocation, to make room for accommodation to new scripts.

4.2 Evolution

In behavioural science, the evolutionary perspective has a number of attractions. It explains the development and spread of forms of organisation, culture, meanings and cognition under limited foresight, and hence limited planning, with no prior intelligent design. In economics and management, evolutionary theory keeps us from the error of an unrealistically rational, magical view of development as the design by somehow prescient or even clairvoyant managers, entrepreneurs and scientists, as well as from the opposite error of institutional or technological determinism, whereby forms of organisation are dictated by external conditions of technology and market (McKelvey, 1982). In the first, managerial actors are omnipotent, while in the latter actors are absent.

Evolutionary theory helps to deal with what in sociology is called the problem of agency and structure, how structure constrains and enables agency but is also produced by it. While characteristics of entrepreneurs and organisations have a causal effect on survival and growth of firms, causality can also go another way, with those characteristics being the result of processes of selection and retention (Aldrich, 1999: 336). Evolutionary theory forces us to recognise both the role of actors, with their individual preferences and endowments, in the processes of variety generation and transmission, and the enabling and constraining conditions for action, in structures of markets and institutions, in the process of evolutionary selection. It forces us to recognise causes of change in organisations ('autogenic') as well as outside them ('allogenic') (McKelvey, 1982). It allows for the radical uncertainty of innovation (Shackle, 1961) and for evident and ubiquitous error and failure in human endeavour.

In evolution, diversity of the units to be selected is needed for selection and differential survival to work. Diversity of genetic endowment is needed to yield new organisms. In biology, this occurs in chromosome crossover in sexual reproduction and gene mutation. Diversity of selection environments yields diversity of species, as shown since Darwin in the divergence of species on isolated islands. Diversity is key in DC and evolutionary theory helps us to understand its role. Of great intellectual but also moral importance, evolutionary theory forces us to accept diversity as an essential element of societies and organisations and their development. The old practice, in economic analysis, of dealing with an industry on the basis of a representative firm is a fundamental mistake. As Hayek recognised, knowledge is dispersed and differentiated.

In evolutionary theory as applied to nature, generation of new variety is generally ascribed to errors in replication, and random, uninformed trials as steps into the dark (mutations). Beyond application to nature, in the methodology of complex adaptive systems, the conduct of agents is modelled in terms of if-then rules. In analogy to chromosomes, these are sometimes modelled as bit-strings of messages sent in response to bit-strings of messages received, and the discovery of rules is modelled as random mutations of values at positions in the string plus random crossover of strings, in analogy to sexual reproduction. How valid or adequate is this, as a model of human learning and communication?

While earlier literature was often based on analogies from biological evolution, in more recent literature (Hodgson, 2002b; Hodgson & Knudsen, 2006) a radical abstraction was made in the definition of universal Darwinism (Dawkins, 1983) in terms of only the overall meta-theoretical framework (Hodgson & Knudsen, 2006: 16) of *variety generation, selection and transmission*, regardless of the diverse ways in which those operate in different areas of application of evolutionary theory.

In this universal Darwinism, *interactors* are constituted by the *replicators*, genes in biology, and selected in or out in a selection environment. When selected in, they transmit the replicators. Hodgson and Knudsen claim that this overall framework applies universally to biological as well as economic, cultural and cognitive systems. In organisation theory, it is needed to explain why some organisations last longer or grow more than others, and why some are imitated more than others (Hodgson & Knudsen, 2006: 6). However, while universal Darwinism gives a useful conceptual orientation of research in not assuming prior rational design, it leaves most of the explanatory work still to be done, in a specification of the processes of variety generation, selection and transmission, in terms of people, cognition, work, management, science, invention, innovation, organisations, industries, markets and institutions.

Competition in markets by firms and in fields of knowledge by scientists, with constraining and enabling effects of institutions, is straightforwardly seen as yielding a process of differential survival and retention of products, practices and ideas. There is plausibility in seeing entrepreneurship and invention as sources of variety generation, and to see staff turnover, training, personnel transfer, imitation, consultancy and firm growth as mechanisms for the transmission of proven success.

However, anyone who has studied socio-economic evolution recognises that in many respects it differs radically from biological evolution. First, evolution requires some stability of the selection environment for selection to work, while the selection environment of an economy is in perpetual shift due to political change, rapid innovation and economies of scale that yield concentration and lobbying power.

Second, how meaningful is evolutionary theory if the notions of interactors and replicators turn out not to apply? To function as an interactor, an entity must have a reasonably cohesive and stable set of components. This is the *ecological* side of evolution (Baum & Singh, 1994). Are ideas and organisations sufficiently cohesive and stable? For organisations, would organisational focus fit the bill? Interactors carry replicators (in biology: genes) that in the *ontogenetic* development of interactors generate characteristics that affect their survival and thereby the replication of their replicators. Can scripts be seen as replicators? This generation of characteristics (in biology: gene expression) takes place in interaction within the interactor, between replicators (in organisations: scripts) and other features of the interactor, as well as with the interactor's environment. Replicators may lie dormant, yielding potential until triggered by conditions. Note that it is not the replicators themselves that determine survival but the characteristics they produce. Replicators may generate characteristics on different levels, including abilities to generate characteristics, depending on the circumstances. That may apply to ideas and organisations. Replicators from surviving interactors are replicated and recombined, mostly in populations of interactors that partake of a common pool of replicators. This is the *genealogical* side of evolution, in the *phylogenetics* of a species. Does that apply to scripts from organisations, in industries?

Third, a complication lies in what is called co-evolution, where the interactors can affect the selection environment to enhance survival in 'niche construction' (Aldrich, 1999). Examples in biology are birds building nests, rabbits digging warrens, beavers constructing dams. There are also several forms of parasitism and symbiosis, such as small fish cleaning the teeth in the maw of a shark. However, in societies, co-evolution is of a different, higher order. Among businesses there are alliances. There is increase of scale and concentration of firms that reduce competition in markets, innovation that constructs new markets and shifts old ones, and protective lobbying that avoids selection by markets and institutions. In politics as well as business, there is political manipulation, rhetoric, censorship or other forms of suppression or evasion of criticism and competition. When such co-evolution goes too far, selection is no longer effective, and evolution breaks down.

In evolutionary theory, there is literature on *punctuated equilibria* in technological development (Tushman & Romanelli, 1985; Tushman & Anderson, 1986; Romanelli & Tushman, 1994; Gersick, 1991). While detecting that phenomenon empirically, this literature did not contain an adequate theoretical explanation. In evolutionary biology, Eldredge and Gould (1972) and Gould (1989) offered the beginning of an explanation of punctuated equilibria, on the basis of allopatric speciation. There, the origin of new species is attributed to a long process outside of, or at the margin of, parent niches, where there are challenges and opportunities for experimentation with novel forms without their being swamped by the dominant species in the parent niche. Punctuation is rare, relative to long periods of stability, because it takes a long process of outside trial and error to establish a new form that is strong enough to turn around and successfully invade the parent niche.

This point of evolutionary 'logic' resembles the principle of generalisation in the cycle of discovery set out above, with its exit to a novel context of application. However, upon scrutiny the underlying logic is different. In evolutionary theory, it is only the criteria of selection that change, offering new challenges and opportunities for survival and reproduction that cause a phylogenetic drift away from the parent population, as interbreeding is blocked by some physical obstacle to interaction. Here, by contrast, the novel environment is a source of novel insights into limitations of existing practice, a build-up of motivation to change and, most importantly, suggestions for novel elements that might be tried out, in hybridisation and novel architectural principles to eliminate problems caused by hybrids. While the shift of environment may be imposed unexpectedly from the outside, when disaster strikes or an invading competence-destroying innovation or disaster forces one to adapt, it may also be undertaken voluntarily and by design, in a deliberate step into a novel context of application.

The problems of evolution arise with a vengeance when applied to organisations.

4.2.1 Evolutionary Organisation Theory

In the evolutionary theory of organisations, organisations are seen as interactors in their environments, of markets and institutions in which they may flourish or flounder, and are members of industries that are seen as populations. Their competencies (McKelvey, 1982) or behavioural routines (Nelson & Winter, 1982) are seen as the corresponding replicators, with industries sharing a common pool of such competencies. In a *lineage* of firms, those are similar by transmission or imitation.

There are several limitations to the application of Darwinian evolution to organisations. The survival of organisations depends on their ability to access and absorb information about markets, technology and institutions. Economy of scale also applies: the cost of a bit of information depends on its acquisition, not on its use and size of the firm, so that in a large firm the costs are relatively lower. There does not seem to be anything similar in biological evolution (Rosenberg, 2000). With organisations, acquired information is transmitted, which would make organisational evolution Lamarckian.

A serious problem for the theory is that organisations may affect or even create the selection conditions they are subjected to, in co-evolution. This yields an argument for libertarians in their plea against government interference in markets.

Garud and Rappa (1996) provide an example, concerning the rivalry between two competing technologies for hearing aids in the form of inner ear (cochlea) implants. There were two rival systems: a single-channel and a multiple-channel device. The first carried less risk than the second, but the second yielded a greater improvement of hearing. The problem was the lack of an objective, independent evaluation of these dimensions, making the choice between them subjective. The same ideas that informed the choice of device also informed the methodologies for selecting between them, so that there were rival evaluation methods. The rival methods were championed by rival commercial interest groups and the stakes were high. The single-channel group argued that the obvious choice was to begin with the low-risk device and step up to the other after its risks were clearer and could be reduced. The multiple-channel group argued that this would not reduce risk but add to it in the process of taking out one device and replacing it with the other. No objective experience was available to back up either claim. Selection conditions are routinely moulded by competitive rhetoric.

Another example is that of the invention of cotton carpets. Their advantage was that they felt good to bare feet, but a drawback was that the pile flattens after walking on it. That could be remedied by vacuum cleaning, but that was not part of quality evaluation. The producer lobbied to include vacuum cleaning in the evaluation procedure, finally succeeded and saved their product.

In organisational evolution there is no doubt much trial and error in entrepreneurial venturing and more so to the extent that the innovation is radical and entails destruction of existing competencies (Tushman & Anderson, 1986; Anderson & Tushman, 1990), technologies and forms of organisation, limiting the opportunity to build on existing knowledge and competence. There are however invention and knowledge development, informed by experience from failures and resulting inferences about where sources of failure may lie and where to look for improvements.

Transmission of novelty entails communication, and through the processes of expression and assimilation, meanings of expressions shift and are added to. In terms of the logic of evolution, this means that variety generation is part of transmission.

How is an organisation replicated, and why is there increasing complexity of organisational forms? As discussed before, in nature and culture there are complex adaptive systems that arise, often spontaneously, in self-organisation, where component systems combine in a higher-level system with new functions. The DNA wrapped up in a cell guides how the cell combines with other cells, under local conditions, in the configuration of an organ. There was increasing complexity in a configuration of specialised organs because specialisation of function enhances efficiency (less use of resources) and increases the scope of response to a changing selection environment, increasing the chances of survival. This also happens in organisations.

The literature on evolutionary theory of organisations allows for connected evolutionary processes on multiple levels of skills, jobs, workgroups or *communities of practice* (Brown & Duguid, 1996) in organisations (Burgelman, 1983), of organisations within industries and of industries in wider socioeconomic systems (Baum & Singh, 1994). It is not always clear what the precise interactors and replicators are, on different levels. Here I focus on organisations as interactors in industries, and in this context several questions become relevant.

The most fundamental question is the extent to which the notions of interactors and replicators make sense in organisations (cf. Nelson, 2008). Unlike biology, in the evolution of interactors in the form of organisations and replicators in the form of scripts or routines and ideas, this does not depend on the survival of the interactors that carry them, as noted by scholars like Nelson (2008). It is not even completely clear what 'failure' or 'being selected out' entails. Whatever it means, competencies and ideas from organisations and scholars may be adopted by other organisations and scholars long after the former have 'failed'. Geniuses are often not recognised, and their ideas are not adopted until long after their death. Ideas can subside into obscurity, lurking in libraries or in online clouds, to be rediscovered or re-evaluated much later. Defunct organisational forms and technologies may be revived.

During the oil crisis of the 1980s, the principle of sailing ships was revived and reimagined with computer-guided aluminium sails. When organisations or scholars fail, whatever that means, some of their capabilities or ideas may still be seen as useful and adopted accordingly. Purported replicators may float around, so to speak, disembodied from their carriers, possibly buried in unpublished documents, before they are replicated. If replicators may be disembodied from interactors, does the notion of interactor still make sense?

In biology, replicators generate, through ontogenesis, the interactors that bear them, but the interactors have no influence on the replicators. By contrast, organisations and individual actors are not only active in interacting with their environment but also engage in cognitive construction, which entails that they develop their replicators, on the basis of experience (Witt, 2005). While interactors may be generated by replicators, they also generate them. According to the perspective of *embodied cognition*, individual interactors develop in inter-action with a variety of other people, adopting and transforming some of their ideas and skills. This also happens between organisations. They are generated by the replicators, not only of any well-defined parent, but from a host of other interactors with greater or lesser 'parenthood'. The notions of 'parents' and 'offspring' become diffused. While in biology there is a clear separation between ontogenetic and phylogenetic development, this is not the case in society (Witt, 2005).

If organisational interactors shape their replicators in society, how far such shaping goes is a key question, and to what extent it reliably reflects selection conditions. Hodgson and Knudsen (2006) recognise that if direct shaping of replicators by their carriers were complete and fast, and would reliably reflect any shift or variety of the selection environment, evolution would break down. Survival would no longer be an indicator of success, and many unproven, worthless or deleterious traits would be imitated, along with favourable ones. In other words, as most authors recognised, for evolution to work there must be some isolation of replicators from influence by interactors, or some inertia of interactors (Hannan & Freeman, 1984). A concern is that replicator shaping may to a considerable extent often reflect more or less erroneously perceived or inferred changes in the selection environment, in ways unproven by selection, and that many unproven, worthless or deleterious traits (are) indeed imitated, along with favourable ones. Here, Darwinism does break down.

To what extent can we meaningfully speak of replication at all? Replication entails the maintenance of the content, properties of a replicator, with only occasional or limited 'copying errors', and without significant transformation of form, content or function. Is the transmission of organisational competencies and ideas sufficiently like that? In communication, significant transformation of meaning generally occurs, in the process of absorption or assimilation into existing mental frames. Such assimilation is not a passive act of copying but an active process of structuring and transformation.

For industries to make sense as populations of organisations, there must be differences as well as similarities between firms within an industry, and possi-bilities for replication that are greater within than between industries. Firms in an industry do share certain technologies and practices, in what Spender (1983) called 'industry recipes'. However, due to imitation and personnel mobility between organisations in an industry, or even between industries, organisational identities may not be sufficiently differentiated and isolated for selection to work (Boyd & Richerson, 1985).

In evolutionary organisation theory, what is failure of interactors under selection? Is it the death of the interactor (organisation, scholar) or another manifestation of failure? In the context of firms, selection arises from competition in markets, which may lead to their bankruptcy, take-over, break-up or management buy-out. Even in the case of complete failure, in bankruptcy, others may adopt some of its capabilities as useful.

In sum, the questions in this section are, among others:

- What constitutes the replicator in organisation theory, in the form of organisation-level competencies?
- How do these yield a cohesive and stable organisational identity?
- How does this yield differences as well as similarities within industries, with more opportunities for replication within than between industries, and some but limited shaping of competencies as a function of experience in environments of markets and institutions?

Evolutionary selection is political, and is shaped or avoided by debate, rhetoric, indoctrination, coalition formation and positions of power and influence (or the lack thereof). Are these to be seen as part of selection or as avoidance thereof? Influence of interactors on the selection environment, in co-evolution, is not unique for organisations, and also occurs to a considerable extent in biology. In organisations, the scope for it seems to be of a different order of magnitude, on the basis of intelligent inference of selection forces and the ability, power and political influence of some organisations to shape such forces, in setting standards of technology, conditions of legitimacy, shaping market structure (e.g. distribution channels) and erecting entry barriers.

One may argue that even though for these reasons selection may be limited or inefficient, no theory is perfect. There is reasonable selection in some markets and institutional environments, and not even the most visionary entrepreneur or scientist, nor the most powerful corporations, nor the most able organiser or rhetorician can completely mould their environment to guarantee success, survival and dominance, and some selective pressure will remain. The limits of co-evolution are not only limits of power, but also cognitive limits. One is not infallible in inferring what structure of selection favours differential survival and growth, for lack of insight in causalities of selection and in opportunities that any change might yield to unforeseeable new innovations that may constitute a threat to incumbent organisations.

Returning to the example of the cotton carpet, the most salient aspect is perhaps that it took effort to alter the selection conditions, even in only one, though crucial, respect, which might have failed, in which case the innovation would likely not have survived. Although selection seems very imperfect, it may still be adequate enough to let this issue pass. In sum, for the sake of argument, I will accept that selection by competition still makes sufficient sense, in markets and scientific rivalry.

Knowledge is not only externalised in speech, documents, software, ostensive activity or role models, but is also embodied in tools, in a general sense including machines, procedures and forms of organisation. In learning to use tools, an apprentice may reconstruct some of the mental schemas behind the design and production of the tool. In organisations and industries, replication of knowledge and competencies is:

– At least partly voluntary and subject to choice: one adopts what is perceived to be successful.
– Partial: one may, within restrictions of systemic coherence, adopt only part of a bundle of replicators carried by a given interactor.
– Subject to decay, distortion, reduction, extension and transformation, going far beyond the copying errors, deletions and duplications of genes in biology.

In other words, replication at the same time entails a kind of variety generation.

In socio-economic evolution there is much trial and error in entrepreneurial venturing, and more so to the extent that the innovation is radical and entails destruction of existing competencies (Tushman & Anderson, 1986; Anderson & Tushman, 1990), technologies and forms of organisation, limiting the opportunity to build on existing knowledge and competence. In socio-economic evolution, there are invention and knowledge development, informed by experience from failures and resulting inferences about sources of failure and where to look for improvements. This is too obvious to ignore or deny, and Aldrich (1999), Foster and Metcalfe and Nelson and Winter (1982), to name only a few, all recognised that next to the blindness of trial and error, there is intentional, deliberate and somehow directed variety generation. According to Foster and Metcalfe, 'The rate of economic progress that we observe reflects guided variation within conceptual schemes that channel explorative, creative enquiry in particular directions'. They add: 'Of course, all variation is, in effect, blind variation, since it necessarily deals with the unknowable consequences of a present decision'.

If the search is guided by inference, I would not call it blind, although it does not spell out consequences. What does it mean that variation is both guided and blind? Little, if anything, in the evolutionary literature, is said of how the guidance or direction of variation works in explorative, creative enquiry. More generally, the generation of variety is the least developed side of evolution in socio-economic systems (Baum & Singh, 1994: 18). According to Hodgson and Knudsen (2006: 11) evolution is blind in two senses. First, 'particular outcomes are not necessarily prefigured or predicted in advance'. I agree with that. However, this leaves open the possibility of an intelligent design of a heuristic path, a logic of discovery, guided by experience, which is likely to yield radical novelty, even though it cannot be predicted what that will be. That is what I argued above, with a cycle of discovery.

As Witt (2005) and Nelson (2008) noted, particularly in organisations there is much pre-practice testing, in thought experiments, debate, computer simulations, prototype and market testing as well as consumer focus groups. Human beings learn such testing and experimentation before practice at an early age, in child's play and sports, and proceed to refine their mental experimentation in later education. Such pre-practice testing would have to be included in the notion of selection. However, that means that some selection is not in the selection environment but internal to an individual or organisation.

In sum, when evolution is abstracted from biological evolution, in universal Darwinism, with only the bare notions of variety generation, selection and replication, without specification of how those processes work, it can to some extent be made to fit socio-economic evolution. The attempt to maintain an evolutionary perspective is useful for developing a coherent combination of internal and external causes of change, and of agency and structure, avoiding both an overly rational view of managerial design and a view of environmental determinism without actors. However, with such a bare, abstracted framework, most of the explanatory work still has to be done. A key question is whether a further elaboration of the framework in terms of interactors and replicators can meaningfully be sustained, and here my doubts are more severe. To the extent that this is a requirement for universal Darwinism, I share the doubts and criticisms of the latter that were voiced before by Witt (2005) and Nelson (2008).

4.3 Governance

External sources of change were present in the DC theory from the outset, in the approach from SCP, where strategy was driven by competitive forces. Later, the emphasis shifted to internal sources, but external sources were never entirely absent. Resources and competencies are built inside the firm as well as adopted from outside or constructed in collaboration with other firms or organisations. The need for that becomes more apparent with the notion of cognitive distance. If cognitive distance in the organisation has to be limited for the sake of efficiency, it entails a form of myopia and some blindness to opportunities and threats, which should be compensated in relationships at a cognitive distance that requires its own DC. In this way, theory of the firm also necessitates a theory of collaborative relations and alliances, on which there is an entire literature.

In governing relations there is a difference between trust and control. They are both complements, as control can never be complete, and trust begins where control ends, and they are substitutes, as more trust can relax control. Together, trust and control aim to achieve reliability.

Reliability is crucial in collaborative relations, in view of environmental, epistemic and behavioural uncertainty. Trust is too large a subject to fully discuss here, and I focus on essentials. The subject is linked to transaction cost economics (TCE). A particular problem in inter-firm collaborative relationships indicated by TCE lies in relation-specific investments (RSI). This is a wider concept than the transaction-specific investments from TCE (Williamson, 1975), because such relationships are not a matter of one-off transactions, but of repeated, adjusted and varied transactions in the process of a relationship. The definition of an RSI is that such an investment has value only in that relationship and is lost when the relationship breaks. In the face of that potential loss, this makes one dependent, and the partner can exert pressure for a greater share in jointly produced added value, with the threat that otherwise they will walk out. That is a strategic liability for the other side, but specific investments are often needed to achieve the novel combinations of innovation that yield higher added value than standard products.

There are solutions to the problem of one-sided dependence. One can have such investments on both sides, in balance, or, if by its nature dependence is on one side, one can share ownership and the risk involved. There can be a virtuous cycle where partners both engage in value-adding specific investments, maintaining a balance of dependence. One can also seek something else that achieves balance of dependence, such as having a monopoly in the product or competence involved. An alternative to sharing is the option, usually taken, of forcing continuity of collaboration by contract or take-over, but that reduces variety, in a focus that is partly shared.

Specific investments are made only when there is a reasonable expectation that the relationship will last long enough to recoup the investment. This collapses the often-used rhetoric of maximum flexibility for the sake of innovation. The goal should not be maximal but optimal flexibility, allowing sufficient stability to invest in a relationship with specific investments but maintaining sufficient flexibility to avoid rigidity. Stability of the relationship does, however, entail temporary exclusion of competition, in conflict with government competition policy.

Examples of specific investments are: location-specific investment in installations 'on the doorstep' of a partner, for just-in-time delivery, in a location where there are no alternative partners nearby; investments in specific instruments or machines; specific training and; getting to know who is who in the partner organisation and who is reliable and supported by bosses and subordinates; and in building trust.

Trust is emotional, because it entails vulnerability, but the emotions can also be positive, belonging to the intrinsic value of a relationship. Trust can to some extent be rational, reflective, as opposed to an automatic, tacit, intrinsic or innate inclination to trust, at least in the group one feels to belong to. It can also be based on a rational analysis of why people might be trustworthy. Discussion on trust is, or should be, less about having trust and more about being trustworthy. This is illustrated in Table 1, which is about intentional trust, not competence trust.

The top half of the table concerns control, the lower half, trust beyond control. In the left half of the table one finds public factors, outside the relationship, on the right half, factors in the relationship. The outside factors depend on institutions, hence location. Control, in the top half of the table, has two forms: affecting the room for action, by contract (outside the relationship) or the power of hierarchy, with its directives (inside the relationship) and hostages. In the top left one finds contracts. This requires a reliable judicial system. Another part of outside control is a reliable reputation system. Reputation is a matter of self-interest: one behaves well not to ruin the chance of a fruitful relation in the future, with the present partner or another. A reputation system can be effected privately by specialist consultants, industry

Table 1 Sources of intentional reliability

	OUTSIDE	**INSIDE**
CONTROL	*narrowing the room for conduct* institutions and contract	hierarchy, directives
	affecting choice of conduct reputation	hostages, incentives
TRUST	general trust, morality, ethics, go-betweens	private trust: family, clan, friendship, community, empathy, identification

Source: Nooteboom (2002)

associations or by municipal government offices that are considered to be trustworthy in their competence to judge, to separate gossip from true reports, and in their intention to do so fairly.

The drawback of contracts is that they take time, can be costly and can signal distrust that calls forth reciprocal distrust, which once settled is difficult to remove. That is not necessarily the case as the contract may not be devised to prevent opportunism but for technical reasons, to document who is to do what, for planning purposes, like the minutes of a meeting (Klein Woolthuis *et al.*, 2005).

In the top right of the table, one finds the institution of an organisation, with a hierarchy, issuing directives and giving incentives, and the instrument of hostages. A hostage is defined as something of value to the hostage giver but not the hostage taker, so that the latter will not hesitate to destroy the hostage when its giver does not honour obligations. It is an ancient instrument, with kings surrendering nobles from the court or family members as hostages. Nowadays it can take the form of competition-sensitive information that needs to be shared for the collaboration, but may spill over to a competitor by accident, or may be appropriated by the partner for competition or the threat of divulging the information on purpose to one's competitors.

Beyond control on the basis of legal institutions, reputation, hierarchy with directives, incentives and hostages, there is trust, beyond self-interest. Outside the relation, the basis for this is generalised trust, as a matter of regional or national culture and morality. The evolution of humanity has bred an instinctive feeling for collaboration, with give and take and an inclination towards benevolence, needed already in hunter-gatherer communities since 400,000 years ago (Tomasello, 2016; Moseley, 2019), but this competes with an instinct of self-preservation that is also engendered in evolution. Benevolence can be part of intrinsic, not extrinsic, instrumental motivation. How that works out depends on regional culture and personal inclination and experience. This is not a matter of either-or: one can value both the intrinsic and the extrinsic value of a job or relationship.

There has been a general decline of public trust and trust in institutions, contributing to the rise of populism and conspiracy theories (Hosking, 2019). That entails more complications than can be discussed here, in an intertwining of economic causes and identity politics (Hosking, 2019: 103). Hosking notes that the decline of trust in public institutions has a double effect that also impacts trust in private parties, such as banks, private healthcare providers, pharmaceuticals, science, consultants and other professionals, in a blind trust by citizens on the basis of the assumption of oversight by public institutions, of many things that the citizen cannot judge, and is now seen to fall short. In the population, there is some distrust of government concerning measures taken around COVID-19, and there is some distrust on the part of government concerning the population's civic conduct.

There is also the possibility of go-betweens (Nooteboom, 2002). They can serve to break through emotional deadlocks and put deliberation on a more sober, rational track than the emotional suspicions that often accompany relations. Relations are often governed by unjustified suspicions, especially in case of the 'Calimero syndrome' of a small, vulnerable partner, who is overly suspicious because of it, residing in a loss frame, expecting and seeing opportunism everywhere. The go-between can relieve misplaced suspicions. They can advise on how to proceed in deliberation. They can serve as a guarantor or monitor, instead of a contract. They may provide the service of safekeeping sensitive information, rather than divulging it in a contract, with the risk of it spilling over to a competitor. Trust is an ongoing process and needs to be guarded against undue suspicion and misunderstandings. Again, as in the provision of a reputation system, go-betweens may be private consultancies or municipal offices.

Table 1 can be used to diagnose a relation, seeing what sources of trustworthiness are absent and present, and for therapy, seeking to add new sources of reliability.

The analysis helps to understand the difference between reliance and trust. Table 1 shows the sources of intentional reliability, outside and inside the relationship. Reliability can be based on control, in the upper part of the table, or on trustworthiness beyond control, in the lower part.

I have used the scheme in a project at the Dutch National Police Academy that focussed on citizens' trust in the police. It turned out in a survey that people had reasonable trust in the intentional reliability and integrity of the police but less in its competence. That is better than the other way around: a police service that is highly competent in its corruption. Intentional trust could not be based on contracts, hierarchy or personal bonding, as that is not the relation between citizens and police. It was based mostly on generalised trust and reputation, for which the media was crucial.

The scheme can also be used to understand differences between countries. It has been used, for example, for a comparison of trust between the USA and Japan (Nooteboom, 2019). In the USA, reliability is largely based on contract, reputation and hierarchy. A disadvantage of a contract and reputation is that they are expensive, yielding high transaction costs, and slow in the building of a contract and reputation. As Fukuyama (1995) claimed, the USA has low generalised trust. Yet while he also claimed that Japan is a high trust society, the Japanese researchers Yamagishi and Yamagishi (1994) showed that generalised trust in Japan is low. There, relationships in business are largely based on hierarchy, in the top right of the table, and bonding in family and clans, in the right lower part. In the Netherlands, I think, all sources are at play, with hierarchy being relatively weak. In both Japan and the Netherlands, American governance is increasingly being adopted, in a juridification of relations, in contracts and litigation, in a more or less autonomous mimicry of the USA.

There is a positive bias in trust, as if it is always a good thing, but trust can go too far, in several ways:

- Trust in untrustworthy people is misplaced; if trust decreases because trustworthiness decreases, that is a good thing.
- Naivety and blind trust in disregarding the possibility or evidence of a lack of trustworthiness.
- Trust out of desperation, when there is no alternative. This connects with Albert Hirschman's recognition of loyalty next to voice and exit. If there is no basis for deliberation, in voice, and no option of exit, in being pinned down or coerced to stay, there is only the option of staying put and making the best of it. In Russia under Stalin, people talked lovingly of little father Stalin despite his blatant terror. Psychologically, it was unbearable to face reality.
- The disadvantage of bonding in family or clan, as indicated for Japan, is that relationships are locked into such clans, excluding diversity from outside, which can be bad for innovation.
- Trust in superiors can go too far, smothering criticism and moral qualms, as in the persecution of Jews under Nazism.
- One can have multiple, conflicting obligations: to job, family, personnel, customers, suppliers, environment, nation, that necessitate disloyalty to at least one, in a crisis, and one can be untrustworthy in other areas by necessity.
- According to the philosopher Nietzsche, benevolence and pity are the result of the power play of the weak to protect them against the strong or exert vengeance on them.
- According to Bernard Mandeville (Copleston, 1964 Vol 5 part I: 188), private vices are public virtues. I would say the duty of benevolence can go too far, eliminating the virtuous power of 'thymos', the urge to excel and perform, and deviate, of the entrepreneur, discoverer, athlete, scientist, etc.

However, one can be honest in some of those conflicts, ask for sympathy, offer recompense or accept retribution. One can be trustworthy in one's untrustworthiness.

Concerning the process of trust, there are questions about how to start but also how to maintain a relationship and, certainly not less important, how to end a relationship in reasonably good faith. In the start of a relationship, suppose the partner is unknown, so that reputation does not work. One may be tempted to start with a contract, but that runs the risk of setting the relationship off on the foot of distrust, which is difficult to turn around. If one has the time, one may start with small investments and up the ante as trust grows. That may be too slow. An alternative is to call in the help of a trustworthy go-between. In ending a relationship, one may spring it as a surprise on the partner, or one can warn them in advance, allowing them to reduce their dependence, stop specific investments and find a new partner. This may help to soften the loss frame of a partner wanting you to stay, that may lead them to engage in vociferous revenge.

The point is that the ability to judiciously engage in trust is one of the DCs.

Trust is obstructed by prejudice of race, culture, religion or nation. This is elaborated in the notion of parochial altruism (De Dreu *et al.*, 2014). That is the phenomenon that people are instinctively inclined to altruism in the group they feel to be a member of, while mistrusting outsiders. That yields an evolutionary puzzle. It is conducive to group survival to practise trust and solidarity in the group, but genes are owned by the individual, not the group. So how would an instinct of parochial altruism be inherited? The hazard for a trusting society is that it will be invaded by opportunist outsiders who ultimately gain ascendance, due to better individual survival. It is true, as demonstrated in the game of hawk and dove, that after a while, when the number of collaborators (doves) dwindles, the opportunists (hawks) begin to lose out on victims. A balance between collaborators and opportunists may then arise, and not all collaborators die out. Yet mistrust, identification and punishment of outsiders by a sufficient number, irrationally at a cost to themselves, is a remedy to maintain a wider society of co-operators. This can be inherited culturally. Sadly, here lies the source of discrimination and exclusion of certain immigrants. That may be fuelled by religious or nationalist rhetoric by dictators.

Parochial altruism hampers the positive value of diversity, as a source of a variety of resources, in exchange, but there is more to it. Thought is always biased, and one always thinks, in part, on the basis of unreflected subsidiary assumptions or ideologies. The best opportunity of escaping that bias is opposition from someone else with a different slant on things. That is why diversity is good for innovation as well as intellectual and spiritual development. As noted, at some cognitive distance immigrants are potentially beneficial.

The solution to the discrimination and exclusion resulting from parochial altruism is to extend the boundary of the group one considers oneself to be a member of. Examples are living in the same neighbourhood or trying to categorise the outsider by some other feature, such as a colleague at work, sharing a sport or task, or being the victim of the same hardship or injustice. For that, it is advisable to integrate immigrants as quickly as possible.

Parochial altruism goes together with group self-serving attributions, where positive properties or actions outside the group are attributed to circumstances, not to positive properties, and negatives are attributed to personal characteristics, while inside the group it is the reverse (Smith & Bond, 1993: 179, 86). A region can have more or less parochial altruism, and this requires attention for the sake of a beneficial turnover of population, with immigrants, for the sake of diversity.

In the process of building and maintaining trust, the theory of mental framing can help, focussing on relational signalling. It proposes that in relations one can be in different mental frames (Lindenberg, 2003). One frame is that of protecting one's resources. It is self-interested, based on an instinct, developed in evolution, of survival. In that frame, one will scrutinise actions for evidence of threat, and is tempted to surrender to suspicion and 'exit' as opposed to 'voice' (Hirschman, 1970). The second frame is that of solidarity, where one is prepared to trust and engage in informal give and take, and altruism, up to a point, from the instinct, also developed in evolution, of wanting to collaborate and engage in empathy and voice. There, when an expectation is unfulfilled, the default is to voice it, with the intent of trying to sort things out and solve problems with mutual effort. If that fails, one can fall back on exit. It can be difficult to switch from one frame of thought to the other: the frame one is in can be robust, especially the one of guarding resources. The solidarity frame is needed for trust. One will observe actions as evidence of the frame the other is in and one will try to prevent the switch away from the solidarity frame. This is the notion of relational signalling. One needs to show with beneficent actions that one is in the solidarity frame, and to bring the partner into that frame and keep them there. (Six, 2005) investigated actions in this frame. Seemingly trivial actions may count, such as failing to respond to an email or treatment of a waiter in a restaurant.

When collaborative relations get adversarial and the partner reneges on collaboration (tat), game theory recommends immediate retaliation (tit): tit for tat. The partner will likely retaliate, and collaboration will stall. Therefore, one should now and then accept and forgive for the collaboration to continue. This is called generous tit for tat. The optimality of this, and the optimal frequency of forgiveness, is demonstrated in computer tournaments.

5 Conclusions

I have tried to show that the DC notion requires further development, tapping from a variety of disciplines and literatures. There is a particular need to develop the key notions of deliberate as well as emergent or experiential learning, interaction with the environment in experiential learning, unpacking the vague notions of 'scanning' and 'entrepreneurial vision', the connection between individuals and organisations, as well as the governance of external relations. This requires using theories of knowledge and truth as well as psychology in the notion of cognitive frames, evolutionary theory, transaction cost theory and even linguistics. A notion from those theories involved in the extension of DC theory is, among others, declarative in terms of procedural knowledge and memory. A process theory of discovery is needed. It needs to show how factors internal and external to the firm interact. A theory of the cycle of discovery (COD) is offered that includes experimentation, in interaction with a new context of application of what already exists. This is an alternation of exploitation and exploration, in single-loop and double-loop learning – a combination of exploitation and exploration. This elaborates on the earlier notions of substitution and transformation of knowledge in the learning process. It shows different types of entrepreneurship: in bringing what exists into a new field of application, where it runs into new challenges to survival and indications of change.

In the COD, change is first a differentiation of the practice or product from memory of previous trials. When that does not suffice for survival in the new context it incorporates elements from the new environment (substitution). Thereafter, more fundamental, double-loop learning occurs, changing fundamental structure to eliminate discrepancies between old and new elements (transformation), and then consolidation in a dominant design. For the learning in interaction between people or organisations there is the notion of cognitive distance, and the role of organisational focus to bring coherence, which can be more or less tight or loose for single-loop and double-loop learning. It includes joint purpose and rules in the organisation, in shared culture. The notion of entropy can be used to formalise the extent, variety and coherence of organisational structure. A theory of the causality of action can be used for the analysis of processes of development, separating out agency from other causal factors. For the structure of processes, and the connection between individual and collective knowledge, the notion of a script can be used. Because of the myopia arising from organisational focus one needs outside complementation, in alliances. This requires the DC of the governance of external relations, including the art of the judicious use of trust.

In summary, the following fifteen DCs emerged:

In general management
- Scenario analysis
- .Seek optimal internal cognitive distance
- Craft, maintain and adapt organisational focus
- Engage in horizontal control

In innovation
- Bring a product into a new market (generalisation)
- Adapt to local context (differentiation)
- Adopt from local context (reciprocation)
- Find inconsistencies and indications for new architecture, and experiment (accommodation)
- Streamline, maximise efficiency of a novelty (consolidation)
- Differentiate for niche markets (product differentiation)

In alliances
- Seek partners at optimal cognitive distance
- Make judicious use of trust
- Balance dependence
- Do generous tit for tat
- Manage position in networks

For further research, more empirical research is a **priority**. Some has been reported in this Element, but much more needs to be done. A complication is that much of it is process theory, which is more difficult to test and model than the optimal outcomes of processes that economists, for example, habitually calculate. A new opportunity has arisen in the form of agent-based simulation, where the actions of individual agents can be modelled in their interaction. I have used it to model the emergence and destruction of trust. That has its own methodological problems. Very rapidly, complexity explodes in trying out different values of the parameters that drive the action, and it soon becomes opaque. Testing the model becomes a problem. A solution is to test aggregate outcomes against statistics, but testing the micro-dynamics that are the goal of the exercise remains difficult. I have tried to test the cycle of discovery empirically, but that remains anecdotal.

In further research, another challenge is to see whether there may be other process logics of change than the COD discussed here.

Concerning external relations, much use has been made of the literature of organisational alliances in this text, but no doubt more can be derived from that literature.

I expect potential in further developing the application of the notion of entropy to the structure and dynamics of organisations.

Another extension is to consider issues of morality and ethics, concerning organisational justice, environmental responsibility and related competencies.

There is a wide scope for applying the analysis to specific organisations or industries. An existing analysis of scientists and science, and related DCs, was left out.

Glossary

Cognitive distance: Difference in knowledge and morality between people and between organisations

Cycle of discovery: A process of innovation, with the stages of generalisation, differentiation, reciprocation, accommodation, consolidation and product differentiation

Dynamic capabilities: Capabilities to effect adaptation or transformation of knowledge, organisational learning, governance of external relations and network position

Declarative memory: Memory of isolated facts, figures, names, places and dates

Deontology: Duty ethics

Differentiation: Adapting a product or practice by differentiating it from the variety of experience

Ethics: Theory of the good life

Eudaimonia: Happiness as practising virtues across a whole life

Game theory: Analysis of action and response of interacting agents

Generalisation: Carrying a product into a new field

Generous tit for tat: Reciprocating defection of a partner, but with occasional forgiveness

Heuristic: A tacit decision practice that is not substantively rational but may be adaptive

Horizontal control: Ask the agent to be controlled how it is best controlled, and lay this down in an agreement

Langue: Intersubjective, synchronic meaning

Morality: Rules for conduct based on ethical behaviour

Organisational focus: Achieving a cognitive distance that is neither too small nor too large to fit the goal of the organisation or parts of it, implemented by the building, maintenance and adaptation of organisational culture

Parole: Subjective, personal, diachronic language use

Procedural memory: Memory of a coherent string of language, with connected ideas, in an account of processes

Product differentiation: Differentiating a product to fit niche markets

Reference: What an expression refers to; truth value of a proposition

Relation-specific investment: An investment that loses some or all of its usefulness when the relationship comes to an end

Reliance: Basing a relationship on a positive expectation of reliability

Reliability: Worthy of reliance by trust or control

Routine: Tacit, habitual practice

Script: Structured routine, a configuration of nodes, governed by subscripts, fitting into an overarching superscript

Sense: How one identifies a thing as something, establishing reference

Strategy: Anticipating the action of an intelligent counterpart

Trust: Reliance even if the trustee has both the opportunity and the incentive to cheat

Utilitarianism: Evaluating an idea or practice by its consequences for the good life

Virtue: Inclination or character trait whose practise furthers the good life

Abbreviations

CD	Cognitive distance
COD	Cycle of discovery
DC	Dynamic capability
IE	Industrial economics
OF	Organisational focus
RSI	Relation-specific investments
RBT	Resource-based theory
SCP	Structure, conduct, performance
SM	Strategic management
TCE	Transaction cost economics

References

Abelson, R. P. (1976), 'Script processing in attitude formation and decision making', in J. S. Carroll and J. W. Payne (eds.), *Cognition and social behavior*, Hillsdale, NJ: Erlbaum, pp. 33–45.

Aldridge, H. (1999), *Organizations evolving*, London: Sage.

Anderson, P. and M. Tushman (1990), 'Technological discontinuities and dominant designs: A cyclical model of technological change', *Administrative Science Quarterly*, **35**/4, 604–32.

Argyris, C. and D. Schön (1974), *Theory in practice: Increasing professional effectiveness*, San Francisco, CA: Jossey-Bass.

Barney, J. B. (2001), 'Resource-based theories of competitive advantage: A ten-year retrospective on the resource-based view', *Journal of Management*, **27**, 643–50.

Baum, J. A. C. and J. V. Singh (1994), 'Organizational hierarchies and evolutionary processes: Some reflections on a theory of organizational evolution', in J. A. C. Baum and J. V. Singh (eds.), *Evolutionary dynamics of organizations*, Oxford: Oxford University Press, pp. 3–20.

Bindra, S., S. Srivastava, D. Sharma and V. Ongsukal (2020), 'Reviewing knowledge-based dynamic capabilities through meta analysis', *Journal for Global Business Advancement*, **13**/3, 273–95.

Bingham, C. B. and K. M. Eisenhardt (2011), 'Rational heuristics: The "simple rules" that strategists learn from process experience', *Strategic Management Journal*, **32**/13, 1437–64.

Boyd, R. and P. J. Richerson (1985), *Culture and the evolutionary process*, Chicago, IL: University of Chicago Press.

Brown, J. S. and P. Duguid (1996), 'Organizational learning and communities of practice', in L. Cohen and L. S. Sproull (eds.), *Organizational learning*, London: Sage, pp. 58–82.

Burgelman, R. A. (1983), 'Corporate entrepreneurship and strategic management', *Management Science*, **29**/12, 1349–64.

Chesbrough, H. (2003), *Open innovation: The new imperative for creating and profiting from technology*, Boston, MA: Harvard Business School Press.

Child, J. (2002), 'A configurational analysis of international joint ventures', *Organization Studies*, **23**/5, 781–815.

Cohen, L. and L. S. Sproull (eds.) (1996), *Organizational learning*, London: Sage.

Cohen, M. D. and D. A. Levinthal (1990), 'Absorptive capacity: A new perspective on learning innovation', *Administrative Science Quarterly*, **35**, 128–52.

Coleman J. S. (1988), 'Social capital in the creation of human capital', *American Journal of Sociology*, **94** (special supplement), 95–120.

Collis, D. J. (1994), Research note: 'How valuable are organizational capabilities?', *Strategic Management Journal*, **15**/510, 143–52.

Copleston, F. (1964), *A history of philosophy,* vol. 5 part 1, Image.

Crossan, M. and I. Berdrow (2003), 'Organizational learning and strategic renewal', *Strategic Management Journal*, **24**/11, 1087–115.

Damasio, A. R. (2003), *Looking for Spinoza*, Orlando, FL: Harcourt.

Dawkins, R. (1983), 'Universal Darwinism', in D. S. Bendall (ed.), *Evolution from molecules to man*, Cambridge: Cambridge University Press, pp. 403–25.

De Dreu, C., D. Balliet and N. Halevy (2014), 'Parochial cooperation in humans: Forms and functions of self-sacrifice in intergroup conflict', *Advances in Motivation Science* **1**, 1–47.

Digman, J. M. (1990), Personality structure: Emergence of the five factor model', *Annual Review of Psychology*, **41**, 417–40.

Edelman, G. M. (1987), *Neural Darwinism: The theory of neuronal group selection*, New York: Basic Books.

Eldredge, N. and S. J. Gould (1972), 'Punctuated equilibria: An alternative to phyletic gradualism', in T. J. M. Schopf (ed.), *Models in paleobiology*, San Francisco, CA: Freeman, Cooper and Co, pp. 82–115.

Flavell, J. H. (1967), *The developmental psychology of Jean Piaget*, Princeton, NJ: Van Nostrand.

Foss, N. J. (2002), 'Edith Penrose: economics and strategic management', in C. Pitelis (ed.) *The growth of the firm: The legacy of Edith Penrose*, Oxford: Oxford University Press, pp. 147–64.

Fukuyama, F. (1995), 'Social capital and the global economy', *Foreign Affairs*, **89**.

Garud, R. and M. A. Rappa (1996), 'A socio-cognitive model of technology evolution: The case of cochlear implants', in J. R. Meindl, C. Stubbart and J. F. Porac (eds.), *Cognition within and between organisations*, London: Sage, pp. 441–74.

Gersick, C. J. G. (1991), 'Revolutionary change theories', *Academy of Management Review*, **16**/1, 10–36.

Gilsing, V. A., B. Nooteboom, W. P. M. Vanhaverbeke, G. M. Duijsters and A. van den Oord (2008), 'Network embeddedness and the exploration of novel technologies: Technological distance, betweenness centrality and density', *Research Policy*, **37**, 1717–31.

Gould, S. J. (1989), 'Punctuated equilibrium in fact and theory', *Journal of Social Biological Structure* **12**, 117–36.

Granovetter, M. S. (1973), 'The strength of weak ties', *American Journal of Sociology*, **78**/6, 1360–81.

Griliches, Z. (1990), 'Patent statistics as economic indicators', *Journal of Economic Literature*, **28**, 1661–707.

Hannan, M. T. and J. Freeman (1984), 'Structural inertia and organizational change', *American Sociological Review*, **49**, 149–64.

Hayek, F. von (1945), 'The use of knowledge in society', *American Economic Review*, **35**/4, 519–30.

Henderson R. M. and K. Clark (1990), 'Architectural innovation: The reconfiguration of existing product technologies and the failure of established firms', *Administrative Science Quarterly*, **35**/1, 9–30.

Hirschman, A. O. (1970), *Exit, voice and loyalty*, Cambridge, MA: Harvard University Press.

Hodgson, G. M. (2002b), 'Darwinism in economics: From analogy to ontology', *Journal of Evolutionary Economics*, **12**, 259–81.

Hodgson, G. M. and Knudsen, T. (2006), 'Why we need a generalized Darwinism, and why generalized Darwinism is not enough', *Journal of Economic Behavior and Organization*, **61**, 1–19.

Hosking, G. (2019), 'The decline of trust in government,' in M. Sasaki (ed.) *Trust in contemporary society*, Leiden: Brill, pp. 77–103.

Janow, R. (2003), 'Shannon entropy applied to productivity of organisations', IEEE Xplore. IEMC '03 Proceedings. *Managing technologically driven organizations: The human side of innovation and change*, 25–29, doi: 10.1109/IEMC.2003.1252225.

Kahneman, D. and A. Tversky (1979), 'Prospect theory: "An Analysis of Decisions under Risk"', *Econometrica*, **47**/2, 263–91.

Kirzner, I. (1973), *Competition and entrepreneurship*, Chicago,IL: University of Chicago Press.

Klein Woolthuis, R., B. Hillebrand and B. Nooteboom (2005), 'Trust, contract and relation development', *Organisation Studies*, **26**, 813.

Kraaijenbrink, J., J. C. Spender and A. Groen (2010), 'The resource-based view: A review and assessment of its critiques', *Journal of Management*, **30**/1, 344–72.

Krackhardt, D. (1999), 'The ties that torture: Simmelian tie analysis in organizations', *Research in the Sociology of Organizations*, **16**, 183–210.

Lachmann, L. (1978), 'An Austrian stocktaking: unsettled questions and tentative answers', in L. Spadaro (ed.), *New directions in Austrian economics*, Kansas City, MO: Sheed Andrews and McMeel, pp. 1–18.

Lakatos, I. and A. Musgrave (1970), *Criticism and the growth of knowledge*, Cambridge: Cambridge University Press.

Lavie, D. (2006), 'Capability reconfiguration: An analysis of incumbent responses to technological change', *The Academy of Management Review*, **31**/1, 153–74.

Leman, P., A. Bremmer, R. D. Parker and M. Gauvain (2019), *Developmental psychology*, New York: McGraw-Hill.

Leonard-Barton, D. (1992), 'Core capabilities and core rigidities: A paradox in managing new product development', *Strategic Management Journal*, **1**, 111–25.

Lindenberg, S. (2003), 'Governance seen from a framing point of view: the employment relationship and relational signalling' in B. Nooteboom and F. E. Six (eds.), *The trust process: Empirical studies of the determinants and the process of trust development*, Cheltenham, UK: Edward Elgar Publishing, pp. 37–57.

Loasby, B. (2002), 'The significance of Penrose's theory for the development of economics', in C. Pitelis (ed.), *The Growth of the Firm; The Legacy of Edith Penrose*, Oxford: Oxford University Press, pp. 45–60.

Malachowski, A. (2013), *The Cambridge companion to pragmatism*, Cambridge: Cambridge University Press.

March, J. G. (1991), 'Exploration and exploitation in organizational learning', *Organization Science*, **2**/1, 101–23.

McKelvey, W. (1982), *Organizational systematics: Taxonomy, evolution, classification*, Berkeley: University of California Press.

Metcalfe, J. S. (1998), *Evolutionary economics and creative destruction*, London: Routledge.

Mintzberg, H. and J. A. Waters (1985), 'Of strategies, deliberate and emergent', *Strategic Management Journal*, **6**, 237–72.

Mokyr, J. (1990), *The lever of riches: Technological creativity and economic progress*, Oxford: Oxford University Press.

Moseley, R. (2019), *Morality: A natural history*, Victoria, BC: Friesen Press.

Narayaman, V. K., L. J. Lee and B. Kamerer (2011), 'The cognitive perspective in strategy: An integrative review', *Journal of Management*, **37**/11, 305–51.

Nelson, R. R. (2008), 'Economic development from the perspective of evolutionary economic theory', *Oxford Development Studies* **36**/1, 9–21.

Nelson, R. R. and S. Winter (1982), *An evolutionary theory of economic change*, Cambridge: Cambridge University Press.

Nettle, D. (2006), 'The evolution of personality variation in humans and other animals', *American Psychologist*, **11**/6, 622–31.

Nooteboom, B. (1994), 'Innovation and diffusion in small business: Theory and empirical evidence', *Small Business Economics*, **6**, 327–47.

Nooteboom, B. (2000), *Learning and innovation in organisations and economies*, Oxford: Oxford University Press.

Nooteboom B. (2004), 'Competence and governance: How can they be combined?' *Cambridge Journal of Economics*, **28**/4, 505–25.

Nooteboom, B. (ed.) (2006), *Knowledge and learning, Vol. I: Fundamentals of embodied cognition, Vol II: Knowledge and learning in organizations*, Cheltenham, UK: Edward Elgar Publishing.

Nooteboom, B. (2009), *A cognitive theory of the firm; Learning, governance and dynamic capabilities*, Cheltenham, UK: Edward Elgar Publishing.

Nooteboom, B. (2019), 'Uncertainty and the economic need for trust', in M. Sasaki (ed): *Trust in contemporary society*, Leiden: Brill, pp. 60–76.

Nooteboom, B., P. M. van Haverbeke, G. M. Duijsters, V. A. Gilsing and A. van den Oord (2007), 'Optimal cognitive distance and absorptive capacity', *Research Policy*, **36**, 1016–34.

Penrose, E. T. (1959), *The theory of the growth of the firm*, New York: Wiley.

Piaget, J. (1970), *Psychologie et epistémologie*, Paris: Denoël.

Porter, M. (1980), *Competitive strategy*, New York: Free Press.

Radnitzky, G. and W. W. Bartley III (eds.) (1987), *Evolutionary epistemology, theory of rationality, and the sociology of knowledge*, La Salle: Open Court, pp. 91–114.

Richardson, G. B. (2002), 'Mrs. Penrose and neoclassical theory', in C. Pitelis (ed.), *The growth of the firm; The legacy of Edith Penrose*, Oxford: Oxford University Press, pp. 37–44.

Romanelli, E. and M. Y. Tushman (1994), 'Organizational transformation as punctuated equilibrium: An empirical test', *Academy of Management Journal*, **37**/5, 1141–66.

Rosenberg, A. (2000), *Darwinism in philosophy, social science and policy*, Cambridge: Cambridge University Press.

Saussure, F. de (1979), *Course de linguistique générale*, Payotèque, Paris: Payot.

Schein, E. H. (1985), *Organizational culture and leadership*, San Francisco, CA: Jossey-Bass.

Schilke, O. and A. Goerzen (2010), 'Alliance management capability: An Investigation of the construct and its measurement', *Journal of Management*, **36**/5, 1192–219.

Schilke, O., S. Hu and C. A. Helfat (2018), 'Quo vadis, dynamic capabilities? A content-analytic review of the current state of knowledge and recommendations for future research', *Academy of Management Journal*, **12**, 390–439.

Shackle, G. (1961), *Decision, order and time in human affairs*, Cambridge: Cambridge University Press.

Shank, R. and R. Abelson (1977), *Scripts, plans, goals and understanding*, Hillsdale, NJ: Erlbaum.

Schön, D. and C. Argyris (1996), *Organizational learning*, Reading: Addison-Wesley.

Simmel, G. (1950), *The Sociology of Georg Simmel*, translation by Kurt Wolff, Glencoe, IL: Free Press.

Six, F. E. (2005), *The trouble with trust, the dynamics of interpersonal trust building*, Cheltenham, UK: Edward Elgar Publishing.

Smircich, L. (1983), 'Organization as shared meaning', in L. R. Pondy, P. J. Frost, G. Morgan and T. C. Dandridge (eds.), *Organizational symbolism*, Greenwich, CT: JAI Press, 55–65.

Smith, P. B. and M. H. Bond (1993), *Social psychology across cultures*, London: Prentice Hall.

Solomon, M. (2006), 'Group think versus the wisdom of the crowds: The social epistemology of deliberation and dissent', *The Southern Journal of Philosophy*, **44**, 28–40.

Spender, J. C. (1983), *Industry recipes*, Oxford: Basil Blackwell.

Spender, J. C. (1996a), 'Making knowledge the basis of a dynamic theory of the firm', *Strategic Management Journal*, **17**, 45–62.

Spender, J. C. (1996b), 'Organisational knowledge, learning and memory: Three concepts in search of a theory, *Journal of Change Management*, **9**/11, 63–78.

Spender, J. C. and R. M. Grant (1996), 'Knowledge and the firm: Overview', *Strategic Management Journal*, **17**, 5–9.

Surowiecki, J. (2004), *The wisdom of crowds*, New York: Anchor Books.

Teece, D. and G. Pisano (1994), *The dynamic capabilities of firms*, Laxenburg Austria: International Institute for Applied Systems Analysis.

Teece, D. J., G. Pisano and A. Shuen (1997), 'Dynamic capabilities and strategic management', *Strategic Management Journal*, **18**/7, 509–33.

Teece, D. (2007), 'Explicating dynamic capabilities: the nature and microfoundations of (sustainable) enterprise performance', *Strategic Management Journal* **28**, 1319–50.

Testa, B. and L. B. Kier (2000), 'Emergence and dissolvence in the self-organization of complex systems', *Entropy*, **2**, 1–25.

Theil, H. (1967), *Economics and information theory*, Chicago, IL: Rand McNally.

Thiel, C. (1965), *Sinn und Bedeutung in der Logik Gottlob Frege's*, Meisenheim am Glan, GER: Anton Hain.

Tomasello, M. (2016), *A natural history of human morality*, Cambridge, MA: Harvard University Press.

Tsoukas, H. and R. Chia (2002), 'On organizational becoming: Rethinking organisational change', *Organization Science*, **13**/5, 567–82.

Tushman, M. L. and P. Anderson (1986), 'Technological discontinuities and organizational environments', *Administrative Science Quarterly*, **31**, 439–65.

Tushman, M. L. and E. Romanelli (1985), 'Organizational evolution: A metamorphosis model of convergence and reorientation', *Research in Organizational Behavior*, in: B. A. Staw and L. L. Cummings, Greenwich Conn.: JAI Press, 171–222.

Weick, K. F. (1995), *Sensemaking in organisations*, Thousand Oaks, CA: Sage.

Weick, K. F. and K. H. Roberts (1993), 'Collective mind in organizations', *Administrative Science Quarterly*, **39**, reprinted in M. D. Cohen and L. S. Sproull (eds.), *Organizational learning*, 1996, London: Sage, pp. 330–58.

Wernerfelt, B. (1995), 'The resource-based view of the firm: Ten years after', *Strategic Management Journal*, **16**/3, 171–74.

Williamson, O. E. (1975), *Markets and hierarchies: Analysis and anti-trust implications*, New York: Free Press.

Winter, S. G. (2003), 'Understanding dynamic capabilities', *Strategic Management Journal*, **24**/10, 991–5.

Witt, U. (2005), 'The evolutionary perspective on organizational change and the theory of the firm', in K. Dopfer (ed.), *The Evolutionary Foundations of Economics*, Cambridge: Cambridge University Press, pp. 339–64.

Yamagushi, T. and M. Yamagushi (1994), 'Trust and commitment in the United States and Japan', *Motivation and Emotion*, **18**/2, 129–66.

Zheng, S. A., W. Zhang and J. Du (2011), 'Knowledge-based dynamic capabilities and innovation in networked environments', *Journal of Knowledge Management*, **15**/6, 1055–151.

Zollo, M. and S. G. Winter (2002), 'Deliberate learning and the evolution of dynamic capabilities', *Organization Science*, **13**/3, 339–51.

Acknowledgements

This Element was invited by J. C. Spender for the *Elements* series of Cambridge University Press. I thank him for his suggestions, and for challenging me with his comments.

About the Series

Business strategy's reach is vast, and important too since wherever there is business activity there is strategizing. As a field, strategy has a long history from medieval and colonial times to today's developed and developing economies. This series offers a place for interesting and illuminating research including industry and corporate studies, strategizing in service industries, the arts, the public sector, and the new forms of Internet-based commerce. It also covers today's expanding gamut of analytic techniques.

Cambridge Elements ≡

Business Strategy

Elements in the Series

A full series listing is available at: www.cambridge.org/EBUS

Printed in the United States
by Baker & Taylor Publisher Services